D1460369

The adoption process in England

A guide for children's social workers

Jenifer Lord with Mary Lucking

700043533845

coramBAAF
ADOPTION & FOSTERING ACADEMY

Published by
CoramBAAF Adoption and Fostering Academy
41 Brunswick Square
London WC1N 1AZ
www.corambaaf.org.uk

Coram Academy Limited registered as a company limited by guarantee in England and Wales number 9697712, part of the Coram group, charity number 312278

First edition published by BAAF, 2008

Second edition © CoramBAAF 2016

British Library Cataloguing in Publication Data
A catalogue record for this book is available from the British Library

ISBN 978 1 910039 47 2

Designed and typeset by Helen Joubert Design

Printed in Great Britain by The Lavenham Press

Trade distribution by Turnaround Publisher Services, Unit 3, Olympia Trading Estate, Coburg Road, London N22 6TZ

All rights reserved. Apart from any fair dealing for the purposes of research or private study, or criticism or review, as permitted under the Copyright, Designs and Patents Act 1988, this publication may not be reproduced, stored in a retrieval system, or transmitted in any form or by any means, without the prior written permission of the publishers.

The moral right of the author has been asserted in accordance with the Copyright, Designs and Patents Act 1988.

Contents

Acknowledgements

I am grateful to the following people who read a draft of the guide and made helpful comments. Benedicta Ali, Chris Christophides, Jeffrey Coleman, Deborah Cullen, Gavin Evenhuis, Fran Moffat, Roana Roach, Andy Sayers. Thank you to them all.

I am also grateful to Erica Bond for her efficient typing and to Shaila Shah for her help in producing the guide.

Note about the author

Jenifer Lord is a child placement consultant in BAAF Southern England. She provides the social work input to the advice and information service in the region, answering many queries from children's social workers and their managers. She chairs a local authority adoption and permanence panel and is an independent member of another one. She is the principal author of *Effective Panels*, BAAF's guide for adoption panel members, the co-author of *Together or Apart?*, a guide on planning for siblings, and the author of *Adopting a Child*, a guide for prospective adopters.

This edition has been updated by Mary Lucking, with thanks to Claire Shepherd, Elaine Dibben, Alexandra Conroy Harris and John Simmonds.

Introduction

This guide is written for the social workers of looked after children who are, or may be, placed for adoption in England.

As a worker in a child care team, you may have little or no experience of adoption work. You will be able to get advice, information, help and support from your manager and from your agency adoption team. However, this guide is designed to take you through the various stages from planning adoption for a child through to contributing to the court report for the adoption order.

The guide aims to complement other more detailed practice guides, which are referenced in the "Further reading" at the end of each chapter. Its emphasis is on what legislation and standards require to be done.

- It outlines what the legislation requires, including case law.

- It describes useful forms and templates.

- It describes good practice and makes suggestions for further reading.

- It includes some flow charts and a list of useful organisations.

- It aims to answer questions which you may have as you get involved in placing a child for adoption.

Two court cases, *Re B* and *Re B-S*, have had a significant impact on the adoption process, although the law had not changed. The Government published guidance (National Adoption Leadership Board, 2014) to assist all those involved in adoption to understand the implications of those judgements.

In March 2016, the Government published *Adoption: A vision for change* (Department for Education (DfE), 2016a), which sought views on a number of proposals to further improve the adoption process. It also published *Children's Social Care Reform: A vision for change* (DfE, 2016b), outlining its vision for transforming the children's social care system by 2020. A strategy document on delivering these ambitions – which may include amendments to legislation and statutory guidance – is expected later in 2016. At the time of writing, the adoption statutory guidance published in 2013 remains the most recent, supported by some self-standing statutory guidance documents which are referred to at appropriate points in this book.

The draft Children and Social Work Bill was published in May 2016 and will come into force in 2017.

In July 2015, the Government published a consultation document, *Special Guardianship: A call for views* (DfE, 2015a), followed by new regulations on special guardianship on 29 February 2016.

How the guide is structured

The guide is divided into 14 chapters. They are arranged in chronological order, to take you through the process from initial care planning to adoption order.

1 Making a permanence plan

Making a permanence plan defines permanence and details the timescales required. It considers the various options which need to be considered before adoption is agreed as the preferred plan. These include: return to birth parents; placement with relatives; placement with long-term foster carers; and placement secured by a child arrangements order, a special guardianship order or an adoption order. The particular needs of sibling groups are described. The role of reviews and of the Independent Reviewing Officer (IRO) and of permanence planning meetings are also described. It considers Fostering for Adoption and concurrent planning practices.

2 Working with the child

Working with the child considers the legislative requirements for involving the child and finding out and considering his or her wishes, feelings and views. It looks at life story work with the child and involving others in this work. It includes children's views on the work that social workers do with them.

3 Working with the birth family

Working with the birth family considers the legislative requirements for consulting and working with the birth parents or guardians and extended family, including a birth father without parental responsibility.

4 The child's permanence report (CPR)

The child's permanence report (CPR) considers the purpose of this form. It takes you through each of the required sections and gives guidance on involving others in providing the necessary information.

5 The adoption panel

The adoption panel describes the membership of the panel and its functions. It gives advice on preparing for and attending panel.

6 Contact

Contact describes the legislative requirements for considering contact at various stages of the process. It includes some practice points about working with the child, birth family and adopters in relation to contact. Different sorts of contact arrangements are discussed.

7 Adoption support services

Adoption support services describes the legislative requirements for considering support needs and the provision of services at various stages. It describes the assessment process, the range of services which must be available, the roll out of the Adoption Support Fund (ASF) and the Adoption Passport.

8 Authorisation to place a child for adoption

Authorisation to place a child for adoption – placement orders and consent describes the process for obtaining a placement order or consent to adoption. It describes and considers the implications of authorisation to place.

9 Finding a family and making a match

Finding a family and making a match considers the family-finding process. It describes the factors which need to be taken into account when considering potential families and the procedure for taking a match to panel. Children's views are highlighted.

10 Making a placement

Making a placement describes the preparation work needed before a placement can be made. It also considers introductions.

11 Placing a child with prospective adopters who live overseas

Placing a child with prospective adopters who live overseas considers the process when the child is to go to a relative. It also looks at the possibility of placing the child with "stranger" adopters overseas.

12 Placing a relinquished infant for adoption

Placing a relinquished infant for adoption describes the process in these particular cases. It considers the involvement of the birth father and extended family.

13 Supporting and supervising a placement before the adoption order

Supporting and supervising a placement before the adoption order describes the legislative requirements for visits and reviews and considers some practice issues. It includes a list of factors which can be involved when some placements disrupt.

14 Applying for the adoption order

Applying for the adoption order describes the process for this and for writing the court report. It describes the court process and the procedures after an adoption order is made.

The guide also includes:

- the values which underpin the National Minimum Standards for adoption;
- Section 1 of the Adoption and Children Act 2002, as amended by the Children and Families Act 2014, including the "welfare checklist";
- a glossary of terms;
- a list of useful organisations.

A list of further reading is provided at the end of each chapter, and often includes books that you can read with children. Any references cited in the text are gathered together in a reference list at the end of the book but preceding the appendices.

Anti-discriminatory framework

The children and their birth families and the prospective adoptive families whom you will work with will be a very diverse group. Under the National Minimum Standards for Adoption, Standard 2 is concerned with the actions the agency must take relating to the child to promote a positive identity and to value diversity, whilst Standard 10 requires that the agency treats people who are interested in becoming adoptive parents and prospective adopters fairly, without prejudice, openly and with respect. Standard 12 requires that birth parents and birth families are treated fairly, without prejudice, openly and with respect.

As workers, you will also be a diverse group and these same factors will impact on how you work with the participants in adoption. It is important that you make use of formal supervision with your manager to discuss your work as well as consulting with others in relation to any factors which you may be less familiar with.

1 Making a permanence plan

The separation of a child from the care of his or her parents is a momentous step, whether or not they have agreed to it. It is vital that, as soon as possible, a plan is made and carried out which will settle the child in a permanent placement. He or she needs to know where they will be living, not just over the next few months but for the rest of their childhood and beyond.

This chapter considers the various permanence options, the particular needs of sibling groups, and the process for making a decision about which permanence option is likely to best meet the child's needs.

What is permanence?

Permanence can be described as:

- a feeling of belonging to someone who is parenting a child day by day;

- an awareness of the responsibility that someone is taking for him or her;

- the expectation of continuing stability in this placement;

- a feeling of security in being loved and valued both for himself or herself and as a permanent member of the family;

- a growing sense of mutual obligations between the child and parent(s) as the child moves towards adulthood;

- recognising the ethnicity, religion, language and culture of the child's birth family;

- acknowledgement and positive acceptance of the birth family and history, with ongoing contact where appropriate;

- becoming a full member of an extended family and part of a wider long-term network of friends and family;

- growing confidence in being able to cope with the wider world, including 'moving on to independence or supported accommodation only when chosen by the young person' (BAAF, 1996).

Timescales

Adoption Guidance July 2013 2.2 specifies that:

> The child's need for a permanent home should be addressed and a permanence plan made at the **four month** review.

This is the second review, held four months after the child starts to be looked after. Adoption may not be the plan at this stage. There are other forms of permanence and the plan could be for the child's permanent placement back at home with parent(s) or with other relatives. Adoption guidance is clear that, although these timescales should generally be adhered to, the paramount consideration must always be the welfare of the child. Where the agency is unable to comply with a timescale or decides not to, 'it should record the reasons on the child's case record'.

The Adoption Scorecards measure the average timeliness of the adoption process for children. The main indicators are:

- A1: average time (in days) between a child entering care and moving in with his or her adoptive family, for children who have been adopted; and

- A2: average time (in days) between a local authority receiving court authority to place a child and the local authority deciding on a match to an adoptive family.

For 2013–16 the A1 target is 426 days and the A2 target 121 days. There are several other indicators including two on the number of approved adopters and how long they wait to be matched with a child.

What are the permanence options?

These are: returning the child to the care of his or her birth parents; permanent placement with a relative or friend; living long-term with foster carers, either the current ones or new ones; residential care; living with a carer on a child arrangements order or a special guardianship order; or adoption. These options are described in turn in the following sections. It is vital that the option chosen meets the individual child's assessed needs rather than fitting a formula, for example, that children are too old to be adopted at nine or that special guardianship is always best if the carer is a relative.

Returning the child to his or her birth parents

A consideration of this must come first. It is the best option, but only if it can offer good enough and safe care to the child and only if it can be achieved within timescales which meet the developmental needs of the child.

A decision should be based on evidence from a thorough assessment of the parenting capacity and potential of the birth parents. You may want to involve a psychiatrist or independent social worker to do some of this work or this may be ordered by the court in proceedings. However, you probably know the child and his or her parents as well as anyone and you should have confidence in your own assessments and in your own work with the child and with the birth parents.

This guide starts from the assumption that this work has been done and that a decision has been made that the parent(s) will not be able to provide adequate care, even with help and support, within the timescales that the child needs it. This fundamental decision needs to be confirmed at a statutory review. It will also be tested by a court which is asked to make a care order based on a care plan for permanent placement away from the parent(s), or, if there is already a care order, a placement order authorising the local authority to place the child for adoption. Where the birth parents have consented to the child's adoption and the agency is not seeking a placement order, this will be tested by an adoption panel, which considers a plan for permanent placement away from the parent(s), but not by a court.

Placement with a relative or friend – kinship care

If a child can't return to his or her parents, consideration should be given to placement with a relative or friend. It can be hard for relatives to come forward to offer care as they often do not want to appear to be accepting that the child will not return home to his or her birth parents. They may also not realise how serious the situation is and that permanent placement away from the parents is being considered. It can cause huge delay for the child if relatives come forward late in the process, wanting to be assessed.

It is important that you try to find out as early as possible and in as much detail as possible who the extended family or close friends are so that you can approach them on behalf of the child. A well-tested and effective way of mobilising the possible resources in the wider family is through a Family Group Conference.

Family Group Conference (FGC)

This is a process where the wider family is involved in making decisions about a child who has been identified as in need of a plan to safeguard and promote his or her welfare. It was introduced to the UK from New Zealand in the 1990s, with the Family Rights Group taking a leading role.

It is a way of empowering and involving family members at an early stage and, well used, should prevent family members putting themselves forward at a late stage in proceedings and possibly causing delay if the court then orders an assessment. The family members obviously have to agree to the need for a FGC, which does involve their recognition that there are problems and that this child needs a plan to safeguard and promote his or her welfare.

A Family Group Conference should be set up by an independent co-ordinator. You will need to check whether your local authority has arrangements for these meetings. You can get more information on the model for FGCs developed by the Family Rights Group from *www.frg.org.uk*. Chapter 4 of the Family and Friends Care statutory guidance (2011) provides further information and expects that all local authorities will offer FGCs, and that those arrangements will be set out in the local family and friends care policy.

However, even if your local authority does not currently have such a scheme, it is important that you contact and involve family members as much as you can. There are great strengths in family placements and a family meeting can help facilitate planning for a child.

- Children often prefer to live with someone who is "family" and who they already know well.

- The child has some continuity, and is in touch with their own family history and heritage.

- Contact with other family members, including parents and siblings placed elsewhere, may be easier.

However, there are also potential difficulties which need to be kept in mind.

- Is this relative able to keep the child safe and to provide good enough care, or are they too close to or too involved with abusive or dysfunctional family members?

- Does the relative accept that abuse or neglect has taken place or do they dismiss or downplay this?

- Inevitably the relative will be on either the maternal (most likely) or paternal side of the child's family. How much do they value the possibly very different history and heritage of the other side of the family? Are they negative or rejecting of it?

- Is any contact which will be promoted likely to be helpful for the child? If it is judged best for particular family members not to have contact with the child, is this realistic and agreed by the potential carer?

Timing of placement

Looked after children must be placed with approved foster carers. However, if the local authority is satisfied that the most appropriate placement of the child is with a relative or friend who is not approved as a foster carer and it is necessary to place the child before that person can be approved under the Fostering Regulations, the relative or friend (known as a "connected person") can be approved as a temporary foster carer for a period of 16 weeks (Regulation 24 Care Planning, Placement and Case Review (England) Regulations 2010). Basic checks must be carried out before placement and a full fostering assessment must be started with a view to approving the connected person as a foster carer before the 16 weeks is up. The period can be extended for a further eight week period if the assessment has not been completed, but only after consideration by the fostering panel, IRO and the nominated officer of the local authority.

Viability assessment

When relatives or friends are identified as potential carers, it is very important that a thorough viability assessment is done quickly. This will not be a full assessment but rather a check to see whether a full assessment is worth starting. The questions described earlier will need to be addressed. You will also need to look at, among others:

- the wider family situation and risks posed to both children and potential carers;

- their understanding of the child's needs and ability to meet them;

- their parenting experience and ability;

- the time and space they have, including the needs of other children they may be parenting;

- Disclosure and Barring Service (DBS) checks;

- health issues.

It will usually be you who does the viability assessment, although it could be a member of the fostering or adoption team or a member of a kinship care team. In certain circumstances (if the child has been living with them), the family member or friend can make an application directly to the court for a special guardianship order. They must give the local authority three months' notice of their intention to apply. If the judge within family proceedings is considering a special guardianship order, no notice is required and the court is likely to direct an assessment within a much shorter timeframe.

Making the decision

Different local authorities have different policies about permanency planning meetings, and the routes to decision making for permanence may be different for different types of placement. The ADM has responsibility for making a "should be placed for adoption" and matching decision, the fostering panel would need to recommend the approval of long-term foster carers for a specific child, and different areas have different decision-making panels or officers for special guardianship decisions. Each local authority will have written procedures that will need to be followed before a permanency plan is settled. If a decision is made not to place the child with a prospective carer, it is then important that a formal letter is written to the potential carer, giving clear reasons why you will not be taking up their offer, if this is the decision.

If birth parent(s) are unwilling or unable to suggest any potential family carers, it is important to record this fact, and it could be a good idea for your legal department to write to their solicitors to say that they have been asked about this and have been unable or unwilling to suggest anyone.

Legal status

A placement with relatives could be as foster carers, or secured with a child arrangements order, a special guardianship order or an adoption order. In a very few cases it may be safe and appropriate for there to be no order. If there is no order, and the carers are not approved as local authority foster carers and are not the child's sibling, uncle, aunt or grandparent, the placement would become a private fostering one if it is intended to last 28 days or more. However, there would need to be careful consideration of the degree of security and permanence which such an arrangement would give a child.

You need to be aware of and understand the department's policy about kinship carers, and the difference between private fostering and alternative orders.

Case law update

In 2013 two cases, *Re B (A Child)* [2013] UKSC 33 and *Re B-S (Adoption: Application of s 47(5))* [2013] EWCA Civ 1146 set out the restrictions on adoption, making it very clear that adoption is a placement of last resort; that it is such a significant interference with the right to a family life of a child and parents that it can only be contemplated when 'nothing else will do'. This means that all other possible placements for a child must be considered before adoption is possible, and adoption must be the only appropriate placement. This becomes particularly important when considering family placements within proceedings, as if a relative comes forward later in, or even after, the proceedings a permanency decision is likely to have to be delayed.

In an extreme example, *Re LG (A Child)* [2015] EWFC 52, a father had refused to give details of his family during care proceedings, claiming that they had been abusive to him in childhood and would not be available to care for the child. In fact, he had not told his family about the child or care proceedings out of embarrassment. When he did tell them, two months after the child had been placed for adoption, they put themselves forward as carers and a special guardianship order was made to the grandfather, the child having to be removed from the prospective adopters with whom she had been living for nine months. To avoid delay, or possible disruption, for the child, it is essential that all potential family carers are traced and assessed as soon as possible within proceedings, as a court is very unlikely to refuse their application to be considered if they come forward later.

Special guardianship is described later in this chapter. Many relatives feel more comfortable with this, compared to adoption. However, the case law described in the section on special guardianship lays down that there should be no presumption in favour of special guardianship for relatives. The legal option must be determined by the needs and welfare of the child and the facts of the case.

A total of 3,520 special guardianship orders were made in relation to looked after children in the year ending March 2015. Recent research (Wade *et al*, 2014) indicates that 85 per cent of SGOs were to relatives; 15 per cent to former foster carers; 17 per cent of the children were not living with the carer before the order was made; 55 per cent were under five. This is consistent with earlier research (Wade *et al*, 2010; Hall, 2008).

Siblings already placed or adopted

These children, whether full, half or step-siblings, are relatives too, even if they no longer have a legal relationship with the child, and consideration should be given to a possible placement with one of them. It would be a good idea to liaise with your adoption or fostering team about contacting these families. If the child's plan is for adoption, or is likely to be considered for adoption, you may want to think about Fostering for Adoption or concurrent planning with those carers, if they are willing and suitable.

Relatives who live overseas

Chapter 11, *Placing a child with prospective adopters who live overseas*, looks at the particular issues which need to be considered when a child may be placed with relatives who live overseas.

Remaining with existing foster carers

This will provide continuity for the child and may well be what the child wants. Permanence could be achieved via adoption, special guardianship, long-term fostering or a child arrangements order. Adoption Guidance 3.14 states that foster carers who express an interest in adopting a child in their care should be given advice about the procedures that will apply in their case. A person who is an approved foster carer and wishes to adopt can be assessed under the fast-track adoption assessment and approval process.

The benefits of continuity and of maintaining a good attachment and avoiding a move for a child do need to be weighted against other factors. The carers may be much older than usual; they may be offering long-term fostering when the child needs legal permanence. These may well be compromises worth making, but this does need to be given careful consideration.

Criticism has been expressed by foster carers feeling pressurised into adopting or special guardianship at an early stage in placements.

It will be important to involve the foster carer's supervising social worker in discussions with the foster carers about plans for the child and about which permanence option is likely to meet the child's needs best. Whilst foster carers should not be placed under pressure to offer permanence, they should be offered the option to explore this.

If a foster carer is very clear that they want to be assessed to offer permanence to a child, this should be thoroughly explored. It will probably be best for someone from the fostering or adoption team to do this. Clear reasons should be given if it is decided not to proceed and, as for potential relative carers, this decision should be made at a permanence planning meeting, perhaps involving someone from the legal department. In one case, the Court of Appeal granted leave to a foster carer to apply for an adoption order even though the child had not been with her for 12 months. The local authority appeared not to have taken her wish to adopt very seriously and had delayed in responding to her request to be assessed.

Foster carers who have had a child in their care for 12 months or more can apply to court for an adoption order without the permission of the local authority. They can apply sooner with the leave of the court or if they have been assessed and approved as adopters and the match for adoption has been to panel. However, if the adoption application is not supported by the agency, the adopters will be limited in the adoption support that they can access. This should be explored with the foster carer/prospective adopter.

Foster carers can apply for a special guardianship order without the support of the local authority if the child has been in their care for 12 months or more, or with the leave of the court.

Long-term fostering

Research indicates that long-term fostering can provide a sense of permanence for some children and young people. Their birth parents retain parental responsibility and may remain in quite frequent contact. Foster carers work in partnership with the local authority and receive a fostering allowance which is not means-tested and may include a fee. The child will receive ring-fenced services available to looked after children.

He or she will remain a looked after child, subject to statutory visits and reviews, which may be felt to be stigmatising by some children. The foster carers will not have parental responsibility; this is shared instead by the local authority (if it has a care order) and the birth parents. The local authority could decide to move the child and so too could the birth parents, if necessary by applying to court for a revocation of the care order. So, legally the placement is not secure, although in practice, with co-operation between all the parties, it may feel so to the child and to the carers.

At child care reviews the placement agreement with the foster carers can be looked at and it may be possible to delegate some more decisions to the foster carers if the placement is agreed to be a long-term one. Section 3.195 of the Children Act 1989 guidance and regulations *Volume 2: Care Planning, Placement and Case Review* (DfE, 2015c) states that 'where the plan is for long term foster care, the foster carers should have a significant say in the majority of decisions about the child's care, including longer term decisions such as which school the child will attend'.

Many agencies take long-term fostering as a plan for a child, the approval of people as long-term or permanent carers, and a match for long-term fostering, to a panel. This might be a fostering panel or a panel called a permanence panel. Long-term fostering plans and matches are not required by legislation to go to a panel although this is fairly widely agreed to be good practice.

The agency decision-maker may sometimes agree adoption as a plan but, if adopters have not been found within a reasonable timeframe for that child, the agency may decide to change the plan to one of long-term fostering.

If long-term fostering becomes the permanence plan, it is important that the carers and the child are clear about this. It will be very important for both to know that this is now the child's permanent family and that there are no plans for him or her to move until they are at least 18 and possibly older (Staying Put). When the decision is made, it is likely to be helpful if a letter is written to the foster carers and also to the child confirming the plan. One child proudly framed this letter and put it on her bedroom wall.

Staying Put is intended to extend children and young people's transition to adulthood within a family and household supported environment, and to ensure that young people:

- can remain with their former foster carers until they are prepared for adulthood;
- can experience a transition akin to their peers;
- avoid social exclusion; and
- can be more likely to avert a subsequent housing and tenancy breakdown.

Local authorities are required to have a Staying Put policy. This should set out the practical, financial, tax and benefit issues (for both the foster carer and the child) which impact on the decision to extend foster care as Staying Put care when a looked after child reaches the age of 18 years ("Staying Put" Arrangements for Care Leavers aged 18 and above to stay on with their former foster carers, DfE, DWP and HMRC Guidance, 2013).

Residential care

This may be the preferred permanence option for a child with very significant disabilities or other very special needs for whom family care is not feasible or appropriate. However, it will need to be clear that family care has been fully explored with, for instance, two carers being paid to offer full-time care to a child in a family setting. Alternatively, it may only become the plan when the agency has failed to find a family for the child or when several family placements have disrupted. For a small group of children and young people, it may offer the best form of care and the one most acceptable to them.

Child arrangements order

A child arrangements order is an order introduced by the Children and Families Act 2014 and replaces the previous residence and contact orders (which themselves replaced custody and access orders). The order can set out the arrangements for where the child should live and with whom they should have contact and when. A child arrangements order lasts until the child is 18, and gives a person named in the order as a person with whom the child should live, parental responsibility for that child for so long as the order is in place. Parental responsibility is shared fairly equally and birth parents with parental responsibility would need to be involved in all important decisions about the care and upbringing of the child. The order determines with whom a child lives, although this too can be shared, and with whom a child has contact. For example, a child arrangements order could specify that the child lives with grandparents but spends every second weekend with parents. The child ceases to be looked after by the local authority, although the authority 'may make contributions ... towards the cost of the accommodation and maintenance of the child' (1989 Children Act Schedule 1(15)). Support can be offered by the local authority although there is no statutory requirement to do so, other than to the child as a child in need.

The main use of child arrangements orders is in private law when birth parents separate. For children who have been looked after, special guardianship (see next section) is more likely to be preferred for the greater security and access to support that come with it.

Special guardianship

This order was introduced in December 2005 under the Adoption and Children Act 2002. Section 115 of the Act inserts new sections on special guardianship orders into the 1989 Children Act. Guidance on special guardianship describes the need for 'an alternative legal status for children that offered greater security than long-term fostering but without the absolute legal severance that stems from an adoption order'.

Special guardianship does not remove parental responsibility from birth parents but it enables the special guardian to exercise their parental responsibility 'to the exclusion of any other person'. The only things which they cannot do, without the written consent of everyone with parental responsibility or the leave of the court, are to cause the child to be known by a new surname or to remove him or her from the UK for more than three months. A birth parent with parental responsibility must also still be asked to agree to an adoption order being made. A special guardian must be asked to agree too.

The child is no longer looked after once a special guardianship order is made. However, if he or she was previously looked after, they and their special guardian(s) must, if they request, be assessed for support services, including financial support. These services equate almost exactly with adoption support services but also include potential (although not absolute) access for the formerly looked after child to leaving care services.

Special guardianship orders are made by a court and can be made in favour of one or more people, who must be 18 or over. They do not need to be married. Birth parents are not able to apply. Special guardianship orders can be revoked, but the thresholds for applying are high, and so they offer legal security even if it falls short of that offered by adoption.

There have recently been reported cases in which a special guardian has been convicted of murdering the child in their care. This raised the profile of special guardianship and of the need to ensure that such permanency orders were only made when an appropriate and robust assessment of the carers had been carried out.

New Regulations (The Special Guardianship (Amendment) Regulations 2016) came into force in February 2016. These require local authorities to assess the capacity of the special guardian to care for the child now and up to the age of 18 years; their understanding of current or future risks posed by the child's parents and their ability to manage that risk; and an assessment of the strength of the previous and current relationship between the child and the prospective special guardian.

Applications

Local authority foster carers (i.e. any foster carers of a looked after child, including relatives who are foster carers or foster carers approved by an independent fostering provider (IFP)) can apply within one year of placement with the permission of the local authority which has parental responsibility for the child, and after one year of placement without that permission.

Others, including relatives, can apply:

- if they hold a child arrangements order;

- if the child has lived with them for three or more years in the preceeding five years;

- if they have the consent of all those with parental responsibility, including the local authority;

- or anyone can apply with the permission of the court.

The court can also make a special guardianship order in any family proceedings, after receiving a report from the local authority.

A special guardianship order discharges a care order. If another care order is made subsequently, the court can either suspend or discharge the special guardianship order.

Recent research (Wade *et al*, 2014) indicates that 90 per cent of special guardianship orders have been made in relation to looked after children; 87 per cent of them are children placed with relatives and 53 per cent are aged under five. Contact orders were made in 30 per cent of cases and supervision orders in 24 per cent of cases; this perhaps indicates that there were quite a lot of concerns about some of these placements. In 24 per cent of cases the child had not lived with the special guardian before the order was made and so these cases were untried and tested. A total of 3,520 special guardianship orders were made in England for looked after children in the year ending 31 March 2015.

There is no provision to take a proposal for special guardianship as the plan for a child, the approval of potential special guardians or a match, to a panel. However, a number of local authorities do take cases to a permanence panel.

Special guardianship has been used by courts to facilitate the placement of children with relatives who live overseas. You will need to discuss this with your legal department. It may be recognised in some countries but will not be in others and may not be sufficient to allow the child entry to that country.

Adoption

Fostering for Adoption and concurrent planning

The change to s.22C(9B)(c) of the Children Act 1989 is intended to cover the practice of placing a child for whom adoption is the likely permanence option with approved adopters who have also been approved as foster carers, on a fostering basis, and who would go on to adopt the child if adoption becomes the plan and a placement order is made (or parental consent given). The legislation also allows for such a placement after the agency decision-maker (ADM) decision has been made.

The legislation does not use the terms "Fostering for Adoption" or "concurrent planning" but covers both scenarios. Since the legislation came into force, we have seen two practices emerge:

- Concurrent planning – this generally follows the pre-existing practice, in which carers undergo the full foster carer assessment alongside the adoption assessment, and are thus eligible to be considered for any child. There is usually a proactive rehabilitation plan in place for the child, although it is expected that most cases will result in adoption. Agencies usually recruit carers specifically for the concurrent planning programme, and children are usually under the age of two years.

- Fostering for Adoption – in these cases, carers usually come forward during the adoption recruitment and assessment process (rather than being directly recruited to a specific programme). Local authorities will usually arrange the temporary approval of the approved adopters as foster carers for a named child only under Regulation 25A of the Care Planning, Placement and Case Review Regulations 2010 (as amended by the Adoption and Care Planning (Miscellaneous Amendments) Regulations 2014). In these cases, the local authority is less likely to have a proactive rehabilitation programme in place for the child, will already have considered known relatives, and will be moving rapidly towards making the ADM decision for adoption and applying for a placement order. In some cases, the agency may already have made the ADM decision before placing the child with dually-approved carers.

The DfE published statutory guidance, *Early Permanence Placements and the Approval of Prospective Adopters as Foster Carers*, in July 2015 (DfE, 2015b). *Adoption: A vision for change* (DfE, 2016a, para 4.13–15) sets out the Government's plans to increase the number of such placements.

Legal effect

An adoption order transfers parental responsibility for the child from birth parents and any others who had parental responsibility, including the local authority, permanently and exclusively to the adopters. It is the only way in which birth parent(s) lose their parental responsibility. The child ceases legally to be a member of their birth family and becomes legally the child of the adopter(s), as if born to them.

The child's birth certificate is replaced by an adoption certificate which shows the adopters as the child's parents. The short version of this will be the same as if the child had been born to the adopters. However, the long version does make clear that the child is adopted. The original birth certificate, with "adopted" typed in the margin, is kept by the General Registrar and can be accessed when the adopted person is 18 (although he or she may well have a copy in their life story book or held by the adopters).

The child's surname (and occasionally even the first name) is usually changed at adoption, the surname becoming that of the adopters. However, the name doesn't have to change if a child wants to keep it, or it could be hyphenated with the adopter's name.

Inheritance is from the adoptive family and not the birth family, although it can be arranged that the birth family leave money in a carefully worded will for the child.

A child who is not already a British citizen acquires this if adopted in the UK by a British citizen. A child who is British at birth will not lose this if adopted in the UK by someone who is not British.

Any order made under the Children Act 1989 is extinguished, such as a care order, child arrangements order or special guardianship order, as is a placement order.

Parent or guardian in adoption law

- "Parent" means each birth parent with parental responsibility for the child. (It would include a step-parent who has adopted the child but not one who has acquired parental responsibility through a parental responsibility agreement or order.)

- "Special guardian" means someone who has a special guardianship order.

- "Guardian" means someone who has been appointed to act in the place of a parent after their death. Only a parent with parental responsibility may appoint a guardian. The appointment will usually only take effect after the death of both parents with parental responsibility. The exception is if the parent who appointed the guardian had a child arrangements order before their death. In this case, the guardian acquires parental responsibility even though the other parent may still be alive.

Using these definitions, these are the people who must be counselled and consulted about adoption plans and whose consent must be sought. Birth fathers without parental responsibility should be counselled if the agency thinks this is appropriate. This is discussed in more detail in Chapter 3, *Working with the birth family*. However, their consent to adoption is not a legal requirement.

Contact and relative placements

Although adoption gives the child a new legal identity, he or she is still, in some measure, a member of their birth family and may well continue to have contact with birth family members. Contact in adoption is described in detail in Chapter 6, *Contact*.

Relatives taking on the permanent care of a child may feel uncomfortable with adoption and prefer special guardianship. However, case law is clear that adoption can still be the right plan for some children placed with relatives.

Other points

The adoption process is described in the rest of this guide. However, a few points can be summarised here.

- Adoptions must be arranged by an adoption agency, unless the placement is made under a High Court order or the parent places the child with a close relative – the child's brother, sister, uncle, aunt or grandparent.

- Children can be adopted up to their 19th birthday but the application to court must be made before their 18th birthday.

- Adopters must be at least 21 (unless a birth parent is adopting his or her birth child in which case they must be at least 18). There is no legal upper age limit.

- Adopters can be single, or can be in a couple living together in 'an enduring family relationship'. They do not need to be married or in a civil partnership. They cannot be related to each other in other ways, e.g. two sisters or a mother and daughter.

- At least one of them must be domiciled in the UK, Channel Islands or Isle of Man or each applicant must have been habitually resident here for at least a year before applying for an adoption order.

- Adopters do not need to be British citizens.

Case law

Key Supreme Court and Court of Appeal judgements in 2013 – particularly *Re B* and *Re B-S* – reiterated the need for adoption decisions to be based on robust analysis of all realistic options, and set out that adoption is a measure only to be pursued where it is necessary for the child's welfare. However, those judgements appear to have led some to believe that the law on adoption had changed, and the number of placement order applications fell considerably. As a result, in November 2014, the National Adoption Leadership Board published a mythbusting guide (www.first4adoption.org.uk/wp-content/uploads/2014/11/ALB-Impact-of-Court-Judgments-on-Adoption-November-2014.pdf) that aims to clarify what those judgements do and do not say:

> *The judgments do not alter the legal test for adoption. Courts must be provided with expert, high quality, evidence-based analysis of all realistic options for a child and the arguments for and against each of these options. This does not mean every possible option. The judgment in Re B-S clearly states that the "evidence must address all the options which are realistically possible". Where such analysis has been carried out and the local authority is satisfied that adoption is the option required in order to meet the best interests of the child, it should be confident in presenting the case to court with a care plan for adoption.*

Statistics

In the year to 31 March 2015, 5,330 looked after children were adopted in England, 4,280 of whom were aged five or under. However, figures from the National Adoption Leadership Board show that ADM decisions and placement orders dropped sharply following the *Re B* and *Re B-S* judgements, although this may have begun to level off. The latest figures can be found at: www.gov.uk/government/publications/adoption-leadership-board-quarterly-data-reports and https://www.gov.uk/government/statistics/children-looked-after-in-england-including-adoption--2.

Disruption

Research (Selwyn *et al*, 2015) indicates that 3.2 per cent of adoptions disrupt (i.e. that 3 in 100 adoptions would be likely to disrupt over the 12 years), and that 'it is probably safe to conclude that the proportions of adoptions that disrupt post-order lies between 2 per cent and 9 per cent'. As in earlier research, this study found that the age of the child at placement was the single most important factor.

Children who were four years old or older at placement were 13 times more likely to disrupt than those who were placed as infants. (p338)

There is more discussion of disruption in Chapter 13.

Planning for siblings

There is comprehensive information on working with siblings in the good practice guide, *Together or Apart? Assessing brothers and sisters for permanent placement* (Lord and Borthwick, 2008). This guide also includes a "sibling relationship checklist" which can be used when assessing a child's relationship with brothers and sisters. The following is a summary of some of the guide's conclusions when planning for siblings.

Brothers and sisters have potentially the longest lasting and one of the closest relationships of their lives with each other. Children need to be thought of in relation to their brothers and sisters, from the point of their referral to children's services departments. Vital decisions are often made at an early stage which will affect whether or not brothers and sisters grow up together or separately.

There are a number of key issues which need addressing in relation to children in need as well as to looked after children for whom a permanent new placement may be the plan. These are summarised below.

- Who are the child's brothers and sisters? This will involve talking to each child and to their parents and other birth relatives, as well as reading any files which may exist for the family. Information gathered should be clearly recorded.

- Consideration needs to be given not only to the sibling group who may be living together but also to whether children could be united or reunited with brothers and sisters living elsewhere. This should include consideration for placement with a sibling who may have been adopted.

- If children need to be separated when they start being looked after purely because of a lack of placements, careful consideration should be given to who is placed with whom, regular contact should be arranged, and consideration should be given to reuniting the children as soon as possible.

- What are each child's assessed needs? A full assessment should be done for each child.

- What is the child's relationship with each of his or her brothers and sisters? An assessment should be done.

- What are the child's wishes and feelings in relation to living permanently with or having contact with each of his or her brothers and sisters?

- Could more work or resources help prevent children being or remaining permanently separated from their brothers and sisters?

- Are there valid reasons for keeping separated brothers and sisters apart or for placing them separately if they currently live together?

- How and by whom will this decision be made?

- If brothers and sisters are to be placed separately, the reasons for this should be clearly recorded.

- If brothers and sisters are to be placed separately or to remain in separate placements, their need for contact with each other should be carefully considered and a contact plan recorded. It should be clear how and when this will be reviewed.

It will sometimes be right to place siblings separately. The Adoption and Care Planning (Miscellaneous Amendments) Regulations 2014 amend the Adoption Agencies Regulations to require agencies, as soon as they commence family finding, to consider whether siblings should be placed together or not, so that the right families are sought from the outset. The assessment of each child's needs should be recorded in the child's case record, which they may wish to see later in life.

Making the plan

Permanence planning meetings

It is important that you and your manager involve others in discussing and formulating a permanence plan for the child. Permanence planning meetings should involve someone from the adoption team if adoption could be the plan as this would in turn trigger a requirement to consider a Fostering for Adoption placement, placing the child with adopters who are also approved foster carers (see page 14 for further information on Fostering for Adoption and concurrent planning, especially in pre-birth assessments). The child's CAFCASS guardian, if there is one, should also be invited. Views and information can be shared and discussed, further work identified and a clear plan made.

Legal planning meeting

There will usually be a meeting involving you, your manager and someone from your legal department to discuss and plan applications for court orders. This will involve consideration, under the Public Law Outline, of whether extended family members have been adequately explored as possible carers for the child.

Child care reviews and the role of the Independent Reviewing Officer

As already described in the first section of this chapter, a plan for the permanent care of a child should usually be agreed at the review four months after he or she started to be looked after. This timetable can only be departed from if it is not considered to be in the best interests of the child.

The plan at this stage may include several options for permanence being explored at the same time, for example, a return to parents, placement with a relative or adoption. This is called "twin-track" or "parallel" planning. It is not the role of the adoption panel to recommend whether the plan should be adoption, except where there is parental consent and the agency is not applying for a placement order. Adoption Guidance 1.6 does allow for the panel to give advice in twin-track cases but this is rarely done and the panel is probably not the best forum at this stage.

The Independent Reviewing Officer (IRO) is independent of the case management and of the allocation of resources. He or she has a duty to ensure that children are reviewed according to regulations and to monitor the implementation of care plans, with the aim of minimising "drift" and challenging poor practice.

In between reviews, there is a statutory duty to inform the IRO about any significant failure to implement decisions made as a result of a review, or any significant changes in circumstances after the review that affect the plan for the child.

If problems in the implementation of care plans are identified, the IRO has a duty to try to resolve them by negotiation with the local authority up to the highest level. The IRO should inform children of their rights to complaints and advocacy services and should assist them to obtain legal advice. If everything else fails and a child's human rights are considered to be in breach, the IRO can refer the case to CAFCASS (see Glossary) so that legal proceedings can be considered to achieve the outcome sought by or on behalf of the child.

Child's case record

Where a review has confirmed that adoption is the preferred plan for the child, Adoption Agencies Regulations (AAR) 12 requires a child's case record to be set up.

This must include, as the documents become available:

- the child's permanence report;
- minutes of the adoption panel which recommended the adoption plan;
- the agency's decision and notifications about the plan;
- parental consent to adoption, if applicable;
- placement order, if applicable;
- the agreement with parents if the child is under six weeks old and there is no placement order;
- minutes of the adoption panel which recommended a match;
- the agency's decision and notifications about the match;
- the prospective adopter's report (previously recorded on Form F);
- the adoption placement report and the prospective adopter's observations on this;
- adoption placement plan.

This information must be kept for 100 years from the date of the adoption order. It can be added to both before and after the adoption order (The Disclosures of Adoption Information (Post-Commencement Adoptions) Regulations 2005 (AIR)). Information which can be added includes:

- information supplied by a birth parent or relative, including photos, letters, mementoes, with the intention that the adopted person may, should he or she wish, be given this information (these should be preserved in their original form);
- information supplied by the adoptive parent(s) after the adoption;
- information supplied by foster carers;
- information that the adopted person has asked to be kept, including their views on any contact.

An agency is not required to keep information which it considers would be prejudicial to the adopted person's welfare or would not be reasonably practicable to keep (AIR 4(4)).

The court process

New provisions were introduced by the Children and Families Act 2014 along with changes in practice following the Family Justice Review. The Public Law Outline for care, supervision and other Part 4 proceedings came into effect in April 2014. The changes are intended to speed up the process for children, and require care proceedings to be completed in 26 weeks (extensions can exceptionally be agreed).

Placement order applications are not subject to the 26 week requirement but should be made concurrently with the care order wherever possible. The subject of assessing and placing with relatives or friends is discussed earlier in this chapter.

The 2014 Statutory Guidance on court orders and pre-proceedings for local authorities can be found at: www.gov.uk/government/publications/children-act-1989-court-orders--2

Writing adoption reports

The Restriction on the Preparation of Adoption Reports Regulations 2005 specifies that adoption reports can only be written by social workers with particular qualifications. The reports are all those involved in adoption work, including the child's permanence report, the prospective adopter's report, other reports for adoption panel, reports on visits to children placed for adoption, and court reports in relation to an adoption order.

Those writing these reports must be:

- A registered social worker, who is employed by a local authority or voluntary adoption agency, and who has at least three years' post-qualifying experience in child care social work, including direct experience of adoption work. "Adoption work" is not defined in regulations but Adoption Guidance 1.13 defines "direct experience of adoption", as being responsible for a child where the agency has decided that the child should be placed for adoption and being personally involved in considering whether the child should be placed for adoption, the matching, placement and review stages of the adoption process, and/or being responsible for the recruitment, preparation, assessment and support of adoptive families. Or:

- A social worker, who does not have three years' post-qualifying experience and/or experience of adoption work, can still do this work provided they meet the following requirements, i.e. that he or she is a registered social worker, who is employed by a local authority or voluntary adoption agency, and is supervised by a social worker who is employed by the local authority or voluntary adoption agency and who has at least three years' post-qualifying experience in child care social work, including direct experience of adoption work. Adoption Guidance 1.15 clarifies that it is not necessary for the superviser to be the worker's line manager; he or she could, for instance, be another manager or someone from the adoption team with the requisite qualifications.

- If a registered social worker is not employed by the agency but is doing an independent piece of work, he or she must have the necessary qualifications and be supervised by someone in the local authority or voluntary adoption agency who also has the necessary qualifications.

- A student on a recognised course can do adoption work provided that they are supervised by someone with the necessary qualifications.

Adoption Guidance 1.16 specifies that, in cases where supervision is required as described above, the supervisor must consider and discuss the draft report and must sign it off before it is presented to panel or court.

National Minimum Standards for Adoption

The National Minumum Standards for Adoption were re-issued in July 2014 to take account of the Children Act 2014.

FURTHER READING

BAAF (1996) *Planning for Permanence*, Practice Note 33, London: BAAF

BAAF (2012) *Special Guardianship: Some questions answered*, London: BAAF

Broad B and Skinner A (2005) *Relative Benefits: Placing children in kinship care*, London: BAAF

Forster M (new edn 2004) *The Battle for Christabel*, Colchester: Vintage Books (first published in 1991)

Fratter J (1991) *Permanent Family Placement: A decade of experience*, London: BAAF

Lord J and Borthwick S (2008) *Together or Apart? Assessing brothers and sisters for permanent placement*, London: BAAF

National Adoption Leadership Board (2014) *Impact of Court Judgements on Adoption: What the judgements do and do not say*, available at: www.first4adoption.org.uk/wp-content/uploads/2014/11/ALB-Impact-of-Court-Judgments-on-Adoption-November-2014.pdf

Schofield S (2003) *Part of the Family: Pathways through foster care*, London: BAAF

Schofield G, Beek M and Sargent K with Thoburn J (2000) *Growing Up in Foster Care*, London: BAAF

Introduction

Section 1 of the Adoption and Children Act 2002 makes the *child's welfare throughout his or her life* the paramount consideration for the adoption agency and court when coming to any decision relating to the adoption of the child. The child must be kept at the centre of all planning and must be involved as far as possible at all stages. This chapter looks at the work that must be done with the child once adoption is being considered as the plan for that child.

This work should flow from work that has been done with the child while he or she was still at home, during the separation from home and family and starting to be looked after and in the period while various plans were being considered. You may have been the child's worker throughout this period or you may have got to know him or her fairly recently because the previous worker left or because the child's case was transferred to a new team. If you have not previously known the child, you will need to read the files covering the earlier period, talk, if possible, with previous workers and carers and meet birth family members. The child may be fairly clear about what has happened so far and why or, and this is probably more likely, they may be very confused, with mixed feelings of sadness, anger and powerlessness. You will need to invest some time in getting to know the child before you can expect them to share their true feelings and wishes and fears with you. You will need to go back with the child over their feelings and thoughts about all that has happened so far before you can begin to discuss the adoption plan. This work is described later in this chapter.

The changes to adoption support (see Chapter 7) should be taken into consideration.

The Adoption and Children Act "welfare checklist"

Section 1 (see Appendix 2) of the Adoption and Children Act 2002 (as amended by the Children and Families Act 2014) lists the considerations that courts and adoption agencies must apply whenever they come to a decision about the adoption of a child.

The Act specifies that the adoption agency and court 'must have regard to' (among others):

- the child's ascertainable wishes and feelings regarding the decision (considered in the light of the child's age and understanding);

- the likely effect on the child (throughout his or her life) of having ceased to be a member of the original family and become an adopted person;

- the child's age, sex, background or any of the child's characteristics which … the agency considers relevant;

- any harm … which the child has suffered or is at risk of suffering;

- the relationship which the child has with relatives, and with any other person … including the likelihood of any such relationship continuing and the value to the child of its doing so.

So, key issues which must be explored with the child are:

- their wishes and feelings about the adoption plan;

- what has happened to them so far and the impact this has had on them;

- the relationship which they have with family members and others and the likelihood and value of these relationships continuing after adoption or if there is no adoption. The child's wishes, feelings and views about this contact.

What the regulations require

AAR 13 requires the agency 'so far as is reasonably practicable' to:

- provide a counselling service for the child;

- explain to the child in an appropriate manner the procedure in relation to, and the legal implications of, adoption for the child and provide him or her with appropriate written information about these matters; and

- ascertain the child's wishes and feelings regarding:

  - the possibility of placement for adoption with a new family and his or her adoption

  - his or her religious and cultural upbringing

  - contact with his or her parent or guardian or other relative or with any other person the agency considers relevant.

Adoption Guidance 2.22–26 expands on these requirements.

> Counselling should help a child – subject to age, background and development – to understand over time what adoption would mean for him or her now and in the longer term. The child should be helped to understand why the agency considers they should not stay with their own family or short-term current carer and why adoption is the preferred option for their permanence. They also need to know about the implications adoption may have for contact with their parents, brothers and sisters, wider family members and others (2.23).

Adoption guidance makes the point that it is essential that counselling is provided by or assisted by someone who can communicate effectively with the child as well as having an understanding of adoption. English may not be the child's first or preferred language and in this situation it will be important to work with someone informed and sensitive who can communicate in the child's language. Children with disabilities will also need someone able to communicate with them effectively. There is helpful information on this in publications listed at the end of this chapter.

Adoption guidance is clear that:

> The agency should not give the child the impression that they are being asked to bear the weight of the decision that needs to be made about their adoption. The child should be helped to understand that their wishes and feelings will be listened to and taken into account. The child's views should be recorded. Where the agency is unable to ascertain the child's views, the reasons for this should be recorded on the child's case record (2.25).

The agency may need to involve a former social worker or members of the child's birth family in the counselling but the Adoption Guidance makes clear that 'the agency remains responsible for ensuring that the counselling meets the child's needs as they develop over time'.

Requirement to provide written information for the child

AAR 13 requires the child to be given written information on adoption. The Local Authority Adoption Service (England) Regulations 2003 requires each local authority to have a "children's guide" to adoption and the National Minimum Standards for Adoption specify that the guide must include information on what happens at each stage of the process and how long each stage is likely to take.

Your adoption team should have a guide that you can use. They may have several, designed for children of different ages. There is also a guide available from CoramBAAF which many local authorities use (Shah, 2012).

Life story work

This is the term usually used to describe the work which is done with looked after children to help them to try to understand what has happened in their life so far and why and to express their feelings about this. This is absolutely necessary, before the child can begin to think about the future and what is planned. This work should be started as soon as possible, certainly from the time that the child starts to be looked after.

Children need to know why they are leaving the care of their parents from the time that this happens, or sooner, if possible. The outcome and future for the child may still be uncertain. The local authority may be clear that adoption is the plan but parents and other relatives may still be fighting to have the child back at home. However, it is important that life story work begins well before the court case is finished and the future is clear. The child needs to be helped to understand and express views and feelings about the following:

- who their family are – this can identify positives as well as negatives about the family;

- how they fit into this family;

- what has happened to them so far – this is likely to include moves and different caregivers before they started being looked after, as well as since; it will almost certainly include very distressing experiences of neglect and abuse;

- why these things have happened – what is reality and what may be fantasy or magical thinking; some children may think things happened because they wanted them to or that they are responsible in some way;

- what they would like for the future, including whom they would like to live with and have contact with.

What children want to be told about their past

Roger Morgan, the Children's Rights Director for England, contacted several hundred adopted children to get their views on adoption, and published the results in *About Adoption: A Children's Views Report*.

These are the main things these adopted children wanted to be told:

1. *why they couldn't stay with their birth family and so were adopted;*

2. *details about their birth family;*

3. *whatever the individual child asks about;*

4. *about their own life before they were adopted;*

5. *where they were born;*

6. *if they have any brothers or sisters living somewhere else, and why they were split up;*

7. *whether they can make contact with their birth family.* (Morgan, 2006)

Individual children commented:

| *If you know what happened you can understand your feelings better.*

| *It's important to know their history – you can't just wipe away parts of somebody's life.*

How can I get started on this work?

- As already mentioned, it is important to read files and reports and to talk to birth relatives, foster carers and social workers who have known the child in the past. In this way you will build up an account of what has happened to the child so far which is as detailed and accurate as possible.

- Invest some time in getting to know the child, if you don't already. Do some low-key fun things together which will start to build a relationship and enable the child to get to know and, hopefully, start to trust you.

- Prepare the child's current carers as they will need to be involved in the work. If they are the child's planned permanent carers, they will be central to it.

- Start to go through the child's history with him or her. You will need to go at the child's pace and to be aware of and sensitive to the way it will almost certainly evoke painful memories. It is important that the child's carer is present during these sessions, to provide reassurance and comfort when necessary.

- If the child is already with the people who are to be his or her permanent carers, a new approach could be to start with the present before moving to the past, then back to the present, finishing with plans and hopes for the future.

There are many useful books on doing life story work, some of which are listed at the end of this chapter. There are also many books written for children which can be used to help them deal with their experiences of abuse, neglect, separation and loss. Some of these are also listed at the end of the chapter.

Involving birth parents and other family members

Chapter 3, *Working with the birth family*, considers the involvement of birth parents and other family members in planning for the child and Chapter 4, *The child's permanence report*, considers their involvement in the preparation of the child's permanence report.

If the child's parents are against the adoption plan, it may be very difficult to engage them in the preparation work that you are doing with the child. However, it may be possible to help them to recognise how important it is for the child to have information about them and about their story. Any information that they can share about the child's early life with them and about their own lives will be invaluable.

It will be useful, too, to involve grandparents and other family members, if possible, in this gathering of information. They may have cared for the child for periods and may remain in contact after adoption. They will have information about the child's parents' childhoods and about the history of the family.

Photos, letters, certificates and other documents can easily be copied or scanned and stored and anything which family members can give or lend should be treasured.

Involving foster carers

The child's current foster carers and previous foster carers have almost certainly got valuable photos, documents and anecdotes about the child, which need to be gathered and recorded.

It will be important to involve the child's current carers in the work that you are doing. They will be asked questions about the issues it raises by the child when you're not there and they will also have to deal with the confusion, sadness and anger which the child may act out as he or she is reminded of all that has happened so far and is prepared for another move. This will be hard work for the carers, who will also be grappling with their perhaps very mixed feelings about the child moving on to adopters. It will be important for you to liaise with the foster carers' supervising social worker so that he or she can be alerted to the possible need to give extra support to the carers to manage that loss and to support the child in their transition to their adoptive family.

Carers often produce comprehensive books or memory boxes for children in their care, with photos and mementoes and details of all that has happened while the child has lived with them. While this is a very important record of the child's life with them, it is not a life story book and should not be confused with this.

Foster carers have a very valuable contribution to make in talk and play with the child about what has happened so far and what is planned and in responding to and coping with what the child feels about this. However, they should not be given the prime responsibility for life story work with a child. This should rest with you, the child's social worker.

Involving others in the work

Previous social workers, teachers, health professionals and therapists may have useful information to contribute to a comprehensive picture of what the child has lived through and experienced.

Professionals, such as current therapists or teachers, may need to know that work is going on with the child as this could well affect the child's behaviour at school or in other settings. However, the child should be involved in this. He or she has a right to know who is being told what and why and to express a view on this. It will be necessary to explain to the child why it might be helpful for his or her teacher, for example, to know that an adoption is being worked towards.

Some local authorities involve a worker, other than the child's social worker, in doing life story work and work around preparation for adoption with the child. This may be a worker who is seen to have particular expertise or who has more time than you to do the work. This may offer the child a good service. However, children do value contact with their own social worker and do, understandably, prefer to share their thoughts and feelings with someone they already know and who knows their family. It may work best if you can make a bid for time to do this work yourself, using any specialist worker to offer you advice and consultation.

Life story book

AAR 35 requires that an adoption placement plan is agreed with adopters before a placement is made. Schedule 5, which details what should be in the placement plan, specifies that there must be a life story book for the child, which should be passed to the adopters within 10 days of the adoption order.

There is thus a requirement for a written record of the information which was looked at in life story work. However, it is important to remember that it is the *process* of life story work that is vital, rather than a glossy book that the child doesn't really understand or engage with. The information should be sensitively conveyed but must be honest. For very young children, the book will be a useful record for the future and for their adoptive parents to go through with them.

Life story work can help children build resilience. It gives them a structured and understandable way of talking about themselves and can provide clarity where there are dangerous or idealised fantasies. It can increase the child's sense of self-worth and self-esteem: many children separated from their family of origin blame themselves for the actions of adults.

It may also be a good idea to prepare a second, shorter photo album for the child with some of the life story book photos, which they could share with friends and family who do not need to know the details in the life story book.

If a child appreciation day (see Chapter 10, *Making a Placement*) is held after a child has been matched with prospective adopters but before he or she is placed, the information and any memorabilia gathered on the day will be a valuable addition to the child's life story material.

It will be a good idea to make a colour copy or scan of the book to keep on the child's adoption record held by the agency in case the book the child has gets damaged or lost.

Copies or scans of other photos and documents given to the child could also be kept as a back-up record by the agency.

Child's permanence report (CPR)

AAR 15, 16, 17 and Schedule 1 require comprehensive information on the child and his or her family and on the child's wishes and feelings, to be included in the CPR. This is the key document which the ADM will use to decide whether or not adoption is the right plan for the child. It is also the key document that prospective adopters will be given when deciding whether or not they want to be matched with the child. It is described and discussed in detail in Chapter 4, *The child's permanence report*.

CoramBAAF's Form CPR contains sheets which are designed to be completed with and by the child, on their thoughts about being adopted, the sort of family they would like, and the people they would like to stay in contact with. These sheets should be completed by the child, if possible, as they are a powerful testimony of the child's feelings and views. This work needs to be undertaken over a period of time as the child's views may change as he starts to understand what adoption means and that he will not be returning to his parents or wider family.

What children say about the work that social workers do with them

Adopted Children Speaking (Thomas and Beckford, 1999) describes research done with adopted children to ascertain their views on a range of issues around their adoption. In relation to the work that their social workers had done with them about adoption, the children emphasised how they needed to go over things again and again and appreciated workers who enabled them to do this.

> *He had to explain it to me a couple of times and then I had my queries … It took me quite a while and I kept asking questions all over again and he answered them.*

> *He kept explaining it to me and he kept asking if I understood.*

Other children would have appreciated more help from their social worker.

> *They should try to let their children speak a bit more, so they're not keeping everything stuck inside them.*

> *They could try and see you a little more often or for slightly more time when they come.*

> *… really help them understand what's going on.*

One child said:

> *Understand the child … I know they would have to know a lot about the child. To know a lot about them could really help. Spend time with them.*

Finally, a young person quoted in a chapter in *Direct Work* (Lefevre, 2008) listed the three most important things she believed social workers need to think about when they're working with children:

> *One would be 'listen to them and let them have their say'. The second one would be 'help them', 'be there for them'. And the last one would be 'communicate well with them and explain things; explain if they don't understand and explain it again and again and again till they do, even though you'd probably get a sore throat, but make sure the boy or girl knows what's going on'.*

FURTHER READING

Argent H (2006) *Ten Top Tips for Placing Children in Permanent Families*, London: BAAF

Cairns K and Cairns B (2016) *Attachment, Trauma and Resilience* (2nd edn), London: CoramBAAF

Cousins J (2006) *Every Child is Special: Placing disabled children for permanence*, London: BAAF

Hammond SP and Cooper NJ (2013) *Digital Life Story Work: Using technology to help young people make sense of their experiences*, London: BAAF

Luckock B and Lefevre M (eds) (2007) *Direct Work: Social work with children and young people in care*, London: BAAF, Chapter 2, Lefevre M, 'Knowing, being and doing: core qualities and skills for working with children and young people in care', pp 21–40; Chapter 15, Burnell A and Vaughan J, 'Remembering never to forget and forgetting never to remember: re-thinking life story work', pp 223–233

Morgan R (2006) *About Adoption: A children's views report*, London: Commission for Social Care Inspection

Rees J (2006) *Life Storybooks for Adopted Children: A family friendly approach*, London: Bite Size/Family Futures Publications

Ryan T and Walker R (2016) *Life Story Work* (6th edition), London: CoramBAAF

Thomas C and Beckford V with Lowe N and Murch M (1999) *Adopted Children Speaking*, London: BAAF

BOOKS FOR USE WITH CHILDREN

Argent H (2004) *What is a Disability?*, London: BAAF

Betts B and Ahmad A (2003) *My Life Story* CD-ROM, Orkney: Information Plus

Camis J (2001) *My Life and Me*, London: BAAF

Foxon J (2001) *Nutmeg Gets Adopted*, London: BAAF

Kahn H (2002) *Tia's Wishes*, London: BAAF

Kahn H (2003) *Tyler's Wishes*, London: BAAF

Lidster A (2012) *Chester and Daisy Move On*, London: BAAF

Sambrooks P (2009) *Dennis Duckling*, London: BAAF

Shah S (2012) *Adoption: What it is and what it means*, London: BAAF

Shah S and Argent H (2006) *Life Story Work: What it is and what it means*, London: BAAF

3 Working with the birth family

This chapter starts from the premise that adoption is being considered as the preferred plan for the child. Chapter 1, *Making a permanence plan*, considers work with birth parents and with the extended family in relation to a possible non-adoption placement within the family. However, practices such as concurrent planning and Fostering for Adoption mean that some children may be placed with prospective adopters on a fostering basis whilst further work is done with the birth family. Some may be able to return to their birth family, although most such placements will result in adoption.

The Adoption and Children Act "welfare checklist"

Section 1 (see Appendix 2) of the Adoption and Children Act 2002 lists the considerations that courts and adoption agencies must apply whenever they come to a decision about the adoption of a child.

The Act specifies that:

- the paramount consideration of the court or adoption agency must be the child's welfare, throughout his or her life;

- the court or adoption agency must at all times bear in mind that, in general, any delay in coming to the decision is likely to prejudice the child's welfare.

The Act specifies that the adoption agency 'must have regard to' (among others):

- the likely effect on the child (throughout his or her life) of having ceased to be a member of the original birth family and become an adopted person;

- any harm (within the meaning of the Children Act 1989 (c.41)) which the child has suffered or is at risk of suffering;

- the relationship which the child has with relatives, and with any other person in relation to whom … the agency considers the relationship to be relevant, including

  - the likelihood of any such relationship continuing and the value to the child of its doing so

  - the ability and willingness of any of the child's relatives … to provide the child with a secure environment in which the child can develop, and otherwise to meet the child's needs

  - the wishes and feelings of any of the child's relatives … regarding the child.

Clearly it is best for children to remain with, or be rehabilitated to, the care of their parents or other relatives if they can 'provide the child with a secure environment in which the child can develop, and otherwise meet the child's needs'. This will have been the aim of social work with the birth parents and the wider family. However, if help has been offered and work done but it is still not safe or likely to promote his or her welfare to return the child to the care of the birth family, you must be mindful of the requirement in the Act to 'bear in mind that, in general, any delay in coming to the decision is likely to prejudice the child's welfare'. The child may not be able to wait if a parent needs a lengthy period to overcome the problems which led to the child being removed in the first place.

National Minimum Standards for Adoption

Standard 12 is about involving the birth family actively in the planning and implementation of the child's adoption. Section 12.1 states that:

> *Birth parents and birth families are treated fairly, without prejudice, openly and with respect. They are kept informed, on a regular basis, of the progress (or lack of progress) of their child's adoption. They are given regular opportunities to raise concerns or questions, which are answered as directly and fully as possible.*

Standard 12.5 requires that 'Birth parents' views about adoption and contact are clearly recorded'.

Independent support worker for birth parents

Standard 12.3 also requires that:

> *Birth parents are given access to a support worker from the time adoption is identified as the plan for the child. The social worker is independent of the child's social worker.*

This point would normally be when a review has confirmed adoption as the plan and before the ADM has made a decision. You will need to talk to your adoption team about this. Some local authorities have specific workers who fulfil this role. Others have arrangements with a local voluntary adoption agency. If the birth parents are very opposed to the adoption plan, they may not take up the offer of an independent worker, but the offer must be made. Bear in mind that even if they don't take up the offer initially, they may change their mind later, so it may be helpful to repeat the offer, and to make sure that the parents have relevant contact details. The worker is there to listen to the birth parent and to offer support. They are not there to do work on the plan. It will be important for you to meet with the support worker, perhaps with a member of the adoption team too, so that you can each be clear what your remit and responsibilities are. If you are considering a Fostering for Adoption or concurrent planning placement for the child and adoption has not yet been confirmed as the child's plan, you should offer access to the support worker at that stage: this is because you are "considering adoption" for the child (Adoption Agencies Regulations 2005).

What the regulations require

AAR 14 requires the agency, 'so far as is reasonably practicable', to:

- provide a counselling service for the parent or guardian of the child;
- explain to him or her
  - the procedure in relation to both placement for adoption and adoption
  - the legal implications of:
    giving consent to placement for adoption under Section 19 of the Act

giving consent to the making of a future adoption order under Section 20 of the Act

a placement order

- the legal implications of adoption.

You must also provide the birth parent with written information on the above.

AAR 14 also requires the agency to:

- ascertain the wishes and feeling of the parent or guardian of the child, and of any other person the agency considers relevant, regarding

  - the child

  - the placement of the child for adoption and his or her adoption, including any wishes and feelings about the child's religious and cultural upbringing

  - contact with the child if the child is authorised to be placed for adoption or if the child is adopted.

Other "relevant" people may include relatives and/or the current carers.

Requirements in statutory adoption guidance

Adoption Guidance 2.16–18 and 2.27–38 gives further advice on the work that must be done with birth parents.

- You need to explain clearly to the birth parents why your agency considers that the child should not be returned to them but should be placed for adoption. This may be difficult to do and will be painful for the parent to hear. However, you will have clear evidence of their inability to keep to a contract of work and to demonstrate that they can offer good and safe care to the child. You may need to involve your manager in some joint sessions if parents are likely to get very angry.

- You need to explain the process for getting authorisation to place the child for adoption, either through CAFCASS-witnessed consent or via a placement order.

- You will need to explain the consequences of authorisation to place. One of these is that any Section 8 orders, e.g. a contact order or a child arrangements order, are extinguished and that the Children Act 1989 contact obligations will no longer apply. There will no longer be a presumption for or against contact. However, plans for contact must be considered and the parent can apply for contact under s.26(2) and 26(3) of the Adoption and Children Act. Once the child has been adopted (or during the making of the adoption order), an order can be made under s.51A of the Children and Adoption Act 2014 requiring or prohibiting contact. Section 51A sets out who may apply for such an order. At the time of writing (May 2016), statutory guidance has not been issued.

- You should encourage the parent to consult their own solicitor as soon as possible and explain their entitlement to legal aid.

- You should take all reasonable steps to ensure that the parent is provided with the opportunity to receive counselling, if they refuse it from you, and that they are offered access to a support worker independent from you. Your agency should have suitable contacts available.

- If the parent does refuse counselling, you should record this, and the efforts you have made to arrange it, on the child's case record. You should also write to the parent's independent support worker, if any, and ask the legal department to write to the parent's solicitor to ensure that they are aware of the situation and are aware of the legal implications of the adoption process.

- You should try to maintain contact with the parent, through their solicitor if necessary, and should be ready to provide counselling should they change their mind and decide to accept this. Experience indicates that some quite hostile parents can eventually agree to work with their child's social worker if attempts are made to resolve the conflict.

- Counselling should be sensitive to the birth parents' ethnic origins and religious beliefs. If English is not their first language, there should be involvement from someone who can communicate effectively with them. This should be a specialist interpreter rather than a family member.

- The wishes and feelings of the birth parent must be recorded on the child's case record. They will be included in the child's permanence report and will also be taken into account during the matching process. It needs to be clear whether:

    - they are willing to consent to the child being placed for adoption and, if so, whether this is in relation to identified adopters only or is a general consent to placement with any prospective adopters chosen by the agency

    - they do not consent to adoption: if this is the case, their proposed alternative care arrangements need to be clearly recorded.

- It will be important to explain to the parent that information about themselves and the child, including health information, will be extremely valuable in helping the agency plan for the child and meet the child's needs.

- You will need to explain to the parent that this information will be shared with panel members, prospective adopters and the court. It will also be disclosed to the child, as part of the information in the child's permanence report.

- You should also ask the parent if they wish to leave information with the agency to be passed on to their child, should he or she request this as an adult.

There is additional information about informing the birth parents relating to Fostering for Adoption and concurrent planning in *Early Permanence Placements and Approval of Prospective Adopters as Foster Carers: Statutory guidance for local authorities and adoption agencies* (DfE, 2014), available at www.gov.uk.

Obtaining information

It is very important to try to get as much information as possible from the birth parents as early as possible. When working with the parents of a child at risk, who may still be at home, it will be important to try to get information on the parents and on their extended family. This needs following up as soon as the child starts being looked after, before the adoption plan has been made.

If parents are opposing the adoption plan and are resistant to sharing information with you, it may be helpful to write to them confirming that you accept that any information they do pass on will not be taken as indicating that they support the adoption plan. It may be a good idea to show your legal department a copy of this letter before sending it.

Parental responsibility (PR)

Parental responsibility (PR) is defined by the Children Act 1989 as 'all the rights, duties, powers and responsibilities which by law a parent has in relation to a child and his property'.

This includes the legal entitlement to make decisions about a child – name, education, place of residence, medical treatment, etc. and, *for birth parents, guardians and special guardians only*, consent to placement for adoption, and to the making of adoption orders.

- The birth mother of a child will always have PR and can only lose it on the making of an adoption order.

- The child's birth father will have PR if:

    - he was married to the mother when the child was born or conceived

    - he was registered on the birth certificate on or after 1 December 2003

    - he has registered a parental responsibility agreement with the mother or has obtained a parental responsibility order from a court

    - he has married the child's mother after the child's birth.

- Anyone who has a child arrangements order (CAO) or a special guardianship order (SGO) will also have PR. A non-parent with a CAO does not have the right to consent or withhold consent to the child's placement for adoption, or the making of an adoption order. The holder of a SGO does have this right, which they share with any parent with PR.

- A step-parent with a parental responsibility agreement or order acquires PR.

Working with a father without parental responsibility

If the child's father does not have PR but his identity is known to you, and you are satisfied that it is appropriate to do so, you should provide him with a counselling service too (AAR14(4)). It is important that every effort is made to identify the child's father and to make contact with him to seek his views.

- You should explain to him and provide him with written information about the procedure in relation to placement for adoption and about adoption, and

    - the legal implications of adoption.

- You should also try to establish his wishes and feelings about

    - the child

    - placement of the child for adoption, including any wishes and feelings about the child's religious and cultural upbringing

    - contact with the child if the agency is authorised to place the child for adoption or the child is adopted.

- You should find out, as far as possible, whether he

    - wishes to acquire PR for the child under s.4 of the 1989 Children Act

    - intends to apply for a child arrangements or contact order or an order for contact under s.34 of the 1989 Act.

A birth father without PR is not automatically a party to court proceedings for placement and adoption orders, and he is not entitled to give, withhold or withdraw his consent to his child being placed for adoption, or to seek the court's leave to oppose the making of an adoption order. However, in compliance with Articles 6 and 8 of the European Convention on Human Rights, courts are likely to be sympathetic to an application by a birth father without parental responsibility to be made a party to a placement order or to adoption proceedings. A birth father without PR will also be entitled to be given notice of any care proceedings. (Cullen and Conroy Harris, 2014)

If the birth mother is against the father being contacted and is, perhaps, refusing to give information about him, directions can be sought from the court about contacting him about the intention to place his child for adoption. It is important to try to help the mother understand why it will be better for the child at least to have information about his or her father. There is further discussion on this in Chapter 12, *Placing a relinquished infant for adoption*.

Where there is uncertainty about who the father is, with a mother perhaps naming more than one possible father, you should consider getting a DNA test done. This is now relatively easy to arrange. Your legal department and medical adviser should have information.

If at all possible, the child should have the opportunity to have information about his or her father and to have relatives on the paternal side of the family explored as possible carers.

4 The child's permanence report

Work will have been done with the child and with his or her birth parents and wider family to make a plan for the child's long-term future care. This is described in Chapters 2 and 3. Once the plan becomes one for adoption, AAR17 requires the preparation of a comprehensive report, the child's permanence report (CPR). Form CPR and *Completing a Child's Permanence Report* are published/made available by CoramBAAF.

What is the purpose of the CPR?

- To enable the adoption panel and the ADM to recommend/decide:
  - whether the child should be placed for adoption (panel will have a role in consent cases only, where the agency is not applying for a placement order);
  - whether the child should be placed for adoption with a particular prospective adopter.

- To provide essential information to prospective adopters when they are first approached about a particular child, to enable them to decide whether they want to proceed with a match.

- To provide important information for the adopted person, both as a child and young person and as an adult, about their background, their early history and the reasons for their adoption.

It is very important to keep in mind these varied purposes when writing the CPR. It is a precious document which will remain with the child and his or her adoptive parents for many years. It must be as accurate and comprehensive as possible and must be written clearly and sensitively. It will contain information provided by a range of people, including:

- the child;

- the child's birth parents and wider family;

- professionals from health and education as well as children's services;

- the child's current carers.

You, as the writer of the CPR, have the responsibility for gathering information and for evaluating and analysing it so that it gives as clear and accurate a picture as possible of the child's needs and of the reasons for the adoption plan. As with all work in relation to adoption, you need to keep the requirements of s.1 of the Adoption and Children Act and the "welfare checklist" in mind. This is described in Chapters 2 and 3 and is in Appendix 2.

Involving the child

Involving the child in the preparation of their CPR is one part of the ongoing work with the child which begins long before this. As described earlier, you will have worked with the child to help him or her begin to understand and express their views and feelings about what has happened so far and about what is planned for the future. The child needs to know that adoption is your plan, even if they also know that their parents disagree and that a judge will make the final decision. They need to know why you think it is the best plan for them. They need to be given an opportunity, as described later, to make a specific contribution to the CPR, giving their views.

The child should see and check their own contribution to the CPR. Adoption Guidance 2.65 also states that: 'Where the child is old enough, they should also be encouraged to confirm that their views have been accurately stated'.

Once adoption is the child's plan and he or she is of sufficient age and understanding, the agency must provide a copy of their children's guide to adoption (Statutory Guidance 1.4 and 2.22).

Involving birth parents

Involving birth parents in the preparation of their child's CPR is, in the same way as it is for the child, one part of ongoing work which will have begun long before this. As described in the section "Obtaining information" in Chapter 3, information needs to be gathered from early on in work with parents. It will be important to check back through files to find out what information is already available, especially if you have recently taken over the case.

Parents who oppose the adoption plan may be unwilling to give information for the CPR. You will need to try to explain to them how much any information they do share, about themselves and about what happened to them in their own early life, may help the child in understanding why they have some difficulties in parenting. They also need to be helped to understand how it will give the child an invaluable sense of their history and heritage.

Given the varied purposes of the CPR, which is a document for the long term as well as the short term, it may be that information can be added at later stages if parents eventually come to some acceptance of the adoption plan.

It is important not to leave sections of the CPR blank. If you have not been able to gather information, you need to explain briefly why and to indicate the efforts you have made, for example, how many letters you have written or visits you have made, to try to engage with the birth parents.

As already stated, birth parents are required to have access to a support worker independent of the child's social worker from the time adoption is identified as the plan for the child. It may be that, if the parent is able to accept and engage with a support worker in this way, this worker will be able to help gain their agreement to provide some information for the CPR. You will need to check with your adoption team about any arrangements which they have for providing these workers.

As described later, birth parents should be given an opportunity to make a specific contribution to the CPR, giving their views. Standard 7.5 states that:

> *Birth parents see and have opportunity to comment on what is written about them or their circumstances before information is passed to the adoption panel or to the child's proposed adoptive family.*

This is confirmed by Adoption Guidance 2.65, which states that:

> *Those parts of the CPR that contain factual information about the birth family should be shared with the relevant family members to enable them to confirm their accuracy and agree to it being passed on to the child in due course. Any such agreement should be clearly recorded on the child's case record. Each of the child's parents should also be shown those parts of the CPR which set out their views and wishes, and given the opportunity, if they so wish, to express these in their own words.*

4

Care will need to be taken when, for instance, parents are in conflict with each other, not to give each information about the other which that person would not want passed on.

Involving others

Wider family

Relatives may well have cared for the child for certain periods. Even if they haven't, they probably know him or her well and can contribute useful information on the child and his or her life since birth and on the family history. Information on the quality of their relationship with the child and on their wishes for contact in the future needs to be gathered if possible.

Foster carers

The child's current foster carers should know him or her very well. It can be extremely helpful if they write something in their own words about what the child is like to live with and about changes they may have observed in the time the child has been with them. CoramBAAF has produced forms which may be helpful. There is a carer's report for children aged 0–9 and one for those aged 10–16 (Forms CR-C and CR-YP). You will be able to access these from your adoption team or from CoramBAAF. Either you or the carer's supervising social worker should support the carer in completing the form as needed.

Education personnel

Teachers and others, such as psychologists and the virtual school head, who know the child in their school or nursery setting will have a valuable contribution to make about the child and about both current and future needs.

Experts involved in assessment work

There may well have been psychologists, psychiatrists or independent social workers involved in assessing the child and the parenting capacity of the parents and possibly of other relatives. You may want to incorporate sections or conclusions from these reports in the CPR.

Information from files and from previous workers

It will be important to check what information is available in files. It may also be possible and will probably be helpful to contact previous foster carers, social workers or health and education workers to check this with them and to gather any additional information which they may have.

What the regulations require

AAR 17 requires that a written child's permanence report is prepared. It sets out what must be included, some of which is detailed in Schedule 1, parts 1 and 3, of the AAR and some of which is detailed in AAR 17 itself. The requirements in relation to the health information that will underpin that section are detailed in Schedule 1, parts 2 and 4.

Is there a format for the CPR?

A form for preparing a CPR is available from CoramBAAF. The 2014 version of the CPR was designed so that it can also be used as the Annex B report to accompany the placement order application, to eliminate duplication of work for social workers. It is available electronically and your manager or the adoption team (or CoramBAAF Publications) can tell you how to access it. It comes with guidance notes, but there is also a more detailed guide, *Completing a Child's Permanence Report* (Dibben *et al*, 2014) which provides more detailed guidance on collecting and analysing the information.

What the report must include (Adoption Agencies Regulations 2005)

Information about the child (Schedule 1, Part 1)

- Factual information about the child, e.g. date of birth, ethnicity, religion, legal status.

- Chronology of the child's care since birth.

- Description of personality and of social, emotional and behavioural development.

- Education issues including any special needs.

- Relationships with birth parents, sibling and others, including:

    – the likelihood of the relationship continuing and the value to the child of it doing so, and

    – the ability and willingness of parents or others to meet the child's needs.

- Current contact arrangements with parents, relatives and others.

- Interests, likes and dislikes.

    It is important that factual information is as detailed and as accurate as possible.

    The chronology of the child must be from *birth*, not just from the time of starting to be looked after. The child may well have experienced many changes of care before starting to be looked after. If there are gaps in your information, make this clear and say why, rather than just leaving a blank.

Information on the child's family and others (Schedule 1, Part 3)

- Current factual information on the child's parents, siblings (including half-siblings) and other relatives. You should include here the outcome of the sibling assessment and, where a decision has been made to place the children separately, give clear reasons so the child and adopters can understand why the decision was made.

- A family tree, including information about grandparents, aunts and uncles and parents.

- Clarification of who the father is and whether he has parental responsibility.

- Chronology of each parent since birth, including educational and employment history.

Again, it is important to give the factual information in as much detail and as accurately as possible. If there are gaps, explain why rather than just leaving a blank.

The sections on the chronology of the birth parents should detail their family history and show how they have become the person they are today.

In this Part, "parent" includes the father of the child whether or not he has parental responsibility for the child.

Additional information required by AAR 17

- A health summary by the medical adviser on the child's health, health history and anticipated future health needs.

- The child's wishes and feelings about:
    - adoption
    - religious and cultural upbringing
    - contact with birth family and others.

- The wishes and feelings of parents about:
    - the child
    - the plan, including religious and cultural upbringing
    - future contact.

- The agency's views on and plans for contact.

- An assessment of the child's emotional and behavioural development.

- An assessment of the parenting capacity of the parents.

- A chronology of decisions and actions taken by the agency.

- An analysis of options for future care and 'why placement for adoption is considered the preferred option' (AAR 17(1)). Agencies should be aware of the *Re B* and *Re B-S* cases in 2013 and the "myth-busting guide" issued by the National Adoption Leadership Board (2014) on the First4Adoption website. 'Social workers must ensure that they address all the care options which are realistically possible and provide analysis of the arguments for and against each option so that they can demonstrate why they have concluded that adoption is the right plan. A Table of Realistic Placement Options offers a format on which these arguments can be clearly recorded' (Dibben *et al*, 2014, p32). There has been no change in the law.

These requirements are described in more detail in the following sections.

Health information on the child

AAR 17 requires, in the CPR, 'a summary, written by the agency's medical adviser, of the state of the child's health, his health history and any need for health care which might arise in the future.'

This summary should be based on comprehensive information about the health of the child and of his or her birth family, which the agency has gathered.

Liaison with the medical adviser

It is really important that the medical adviser in your agency is involved **as soon as possible** in checking the health information on the child and his or her family and in deciding whether a medical examination of the child is necessary. He or she needs to be working on this at the same time as you are writing the CPR. There should be a system for this and the agency adviser to the adoption panel is probably the best person to check this with.

Gathering health information on the child

AAR 15 specifies that, although arrangements should be made 'for the child to be examined by a registered medical practitioner', an examination is *not* necessary if this is the advice of the medical adviser *or* if 'the child is of sufficient understanding to make an informed decision and refuses to submit to the examination or other tests'.

Subject to the child's agreement, the medical adviser may arrange for additional tests or examinations to be carried out.

Whether a medical examination of the child takes place at this stage or not, the medical adviser must have full information, as specified in Schedule 1, Part 2 of the AAR, on which to write the health summary for the CPR.

This must include:

- neonatal information about the birth;
- details of serious illness, disability and treatments;
- a physical and developmental assessment;
- a school health history for a school-aged child;
- the impact of the child's physical and mental health and medical history on his or her development.

Gathering health information on the child's birth family

AAR 16 requires, so far as is reasonably practicable, health information to be obtained about the child's family. This is detailed in Schedule 1, Part 4 of the AAR.

This must include:

- a health history of each birth parent, including details of any hereditary conditions;
- a health history of the child's siblings;
- a summary of the mother's obstetric history;
- current health, including any treatment and prognosis.

Are forms for the health reports available?

CoramBAAF has produced health forms in relation to:

- a child aged 0–9 (*Form RHA–C*)
- a young person aged over 10 (*Form RHA–YP*)
- obstetric report on the mother and neonatal report on the child (*Forms M and B*)
- health report on a birth parent (*Form PH*)
- carer's report (*Form CR–C: Profile of behavioural and emotional well-being of a child aged 0–9*)

- carer's report (*Form CR–YP*: Profile of behavioural and emotional well-being of a young person aged over 10)
- review health assessment (child/young person) (*Form RHA–C* for a child 0–9, and *Form RHA-YP* for a young person aged over 10).

The use of these forms is clearly described in Practice Note 47, *Using the BAAF Health Assessment Forms*. Your adoption team and medical adviser should have a copy of this; if not, it is available on www.corambaaf.org.uk in the members' area.

Consent from birth parents to medical information being obtained and shared

In order to complete a comprehensive and holistic health assessment and health care plan for a child, it may be necessary to access the child's and the birth parents' health records, or to contact the relevant health professional. Parental consent is needed to obtain health information from these sources.

You will need to liaise with the medical adviser and with the agency adviser to panel about this.

Practice Note 47, *Using the BAAF Health Assessment Forms*, discusses consent issues. CoramBAAF has also produced a consent form, which can be used.

The wishes and feelings of the child

These must be gathered and recorded, as far as is reasonably practicable, about:

- the possibility of placement for adoption with a new family and his or her adoption;
- his or her religious and cultural upbringing;
- contact with his or her parent or guardian or other relative or with any other person the agency considers relevant.

CoramBAAF's Form CPR has a section which could be printed out and used with the child so that he or she can record their views in their own words. It is important not to leave this section blank. If you have been unable to get the child to contribute anything, detail briefly the efforts you have made to do so. You may find that the child has expressed his/her views in other ways, perhaps to a foster carer or during contact sessions, and that should be recorded. Do not use this section for your views on what you think the child might be feeling: there is a separate section for your analysis of the child's views.

The wishes and feelings of the child's parent or guardian and any other relevant person

This should include the child's father, even if he does not have parental responsibility, if his identity is known to you and if it has been decided that it is appropriate to involve him in the adoption plan and to counsel him. It should also include anyone else whose views would be helpful, for example, other relatives. You will need to record the reasons for any decision *not* to involve the father.

Views should be sought as far as is reasonably practicable, and included in the CPR about:

- the child;
- the placement of the child for adoption and his or her adoption, including their wishes and feelings about the child's religion and cultural upbringing;
- contact with the child if the child is authorised to be placed for adoption or is adopted.

CoramBAAF's Form CPR has a section that could be printed out and used with each birth parent so that he or she can record their views in their own words. It is important not to leave this section blank. If you have been unable to engage with the birth parent and to get them to contribute anything, detail briefly the efforts you have made and the reasons the parent has given for not contributing. Parents may prefer to write a separate letter or statement rather than completing Form CPR and this is fine.

The views of the agency about the child's need for contact with members of his or her birth family or others and the arrangements the agency proposes in relation to contact

You must keep in mind the requirement in s.1 of the Adoption and Children Act, to have regard to 'the relationship which the child has with relatives' and with other relevant people and 'the likelihood of any such relationship continuing and the value to the child of its doing so'.

You will have gathered the views of the child and of birth relatives and others about contact after placement and after adoption. You may also have the views of experts who have done assessments and of the children's guardian. However, the local authority is required to come to a view about future contact arrangements. Who, if anyone, should have contact with the child? Should contact be direct or indirect? How often should it happen? How will it be reviewed in future as the child's needs change? You should detail and evidence why this particular child needs the contact which is being proposed.

Where the adoption panel considers the adoption plan (i.e. only where there is parental consent and the local authority is not applying for a placement order), it must consider and may give advice to the agency about the proposed arrangements for contact. Later in the process, when prospective adopters are identified, their views will need to be taken into account. However, at this stage there must be a plan about proposed contact arrangements included in the CPR.

From the point that authorisation to place for adoption is obtained, either by the making of a placement order or by CAFCASS-witnessed consent, there is no longer a presumption for or against contact with birth family members. AAR 45.2 removes the general duty in the Children Act 1989 to promote contact. Each child's needs for contact should be individually considered. The Children and Families Act 2014 introduced a new s.51(2) to the Adoption and Children Act 2002 which allows the court, before making an adoption order, to consider whether there should be any order made about contact.

There is a fuller discussion of issues around contact in Chapter 6, *Contact*.

An assessment of the child's emotional and behavioural development and any related needs

You will have gathered information on the child's emotional and behavioural development and other needs from many sources including the child himself or herself, their parents and other relatives, their current and previous carers, their school health professionals, any therapists involved and anyone who has specifically assessed their development and needs. This information needs to be reviewed, analysed and discussed so that an accurate and comprehensive assessment can be included in the CPR for the benefit of the panel and of prospective adopters. The CoramBAAF Forms CR-C and CR-YP, mentioned earlier in this chapter can be referred to.

An assessment of the parenting capacity of the child's parents

The CPR will contain information on the quality of care the child received at home and on the reasons for him or her being looked after by the local authority. There may well have been assessments of the parents' parenting capacity by psychiatrists and/or assessment centres. These should be summarised here and it may be helpful to quote the conclusions of the specialists who have been consulted. However, experts may sometimes come to differing conclusions. Even if they don't, it is for your agency to weigh up the evidence, make an assessment and come to a conclusion about the parents' ability to meet the child's needs. This should be clearly stated in this section.

A chronology of the decision and actions taken by the agency with respect to the child

This should summarise the care planning process and the main steps that led eventually to the current plan for adoption. It should include all the moves and changes of carer experienced by the child to date, including parents and other birth family members, and state briefly the reasons for any move or change in placement. It should not be a list of every contact with the family but should draw out from this work an analysis of why adoption has become the plan.

An analysis of the options for the future care of the child which have been considered by the agency and why placement for adoption is considered the preferred option

This is an important section. It should consider the various options for the future care of the child and should indicate why none reasonably meets the child's long-term needs and why adoption does (see earlier in this chapter on the *Re B* and *Re B-S* cases).

The options are:

- return home to parent(s), with support where necessary;

- long-term placement with the child's wider family, either with no order, as a long-term fostering arrangement, or under a child arrangements order or special guardianship order;

- long-term placement with the child's current foster carers, either as a continuing fostering arrangement or under a child arrangements order or special guardianship order;

- long-term placement with new carers under a fostering arrangement (which could, perhaps, become a child arrangements order or special guardianship order in the future);

- residential care;

- adoption (this could be with the current carer, a relative or an as yet unidentified prospective adopter).

Implications for the CPR of the disclosure regulations

Sections 56–65 and 79 of the Adoption and Children Act and the Disclosure of Adoption Information (Post Commencement Adoptions) Regulations 2005 set out the legal framework for managing and disclosing information in relation to adoptions which have taken place on or after 30 December 2005.

The child's prospective adoptive parents must be given a copy of the CPR when they are being matched with the child. They will keep this and will probably share information from it with the child in an age-appropriate way as the child grows up. The agency must also keep the CPR and all the other information in the child's adoption record for 100 years from the date of the adoption order. An adopted adult has the right to receive from the agency a copy of everything that their adoptive parents were given at the time they were placed for adoption. Thus, at 18 or later, an adopted person must be given a copy of their CPR if they request it from the agency.

The CPR will contain identifying information concerning the birth family but this is considered to be the child's information to have and should not be anonymised. However, it is very important that information is as accurate as possible and that the CPR is written with a view to it being read by the child when an adult. Birth parents and other relatives should be given the opportunity to see and check the information about them and should, if possible, give their agreement to it being shared with the child. However, they do not have a veto on information in the CPR and it is the child's welfare throughout his or her life which is the paramount consideration in all decisions.

FURTHER READING

BAAF (2004) *Using the BAAF Health Assessment Forms*, Practice Note 47, London: BAAF

Dibben E, Bugarski L, Probert N and Wilson J (2014) *Completing a Child's Permanence Report: A guide to collecting and analysing information for a Child's Permanence Report (CPR) England*, London: BAAF

National Adoption Leadership Board (2014) *Impact of Court Judgments on Adoption: What the judgments do and do not say*, London: National Adoption Leadership Board, available at: www.first4adoption.org.uk/wp-content/uploads/2014/11/ALB-Impact-of-Court-Judgments-on-Adoption-November-2014.pdf

5 The adoption panel

You will need to attend the panel when consideration is given to whether your child should be placed for adoption: panel only considers whether a child should be placed for adoption in cases where there is parental consent to adoption and the agency will not apply for a placement order.

Non-consent cases go directly to the agency decision-maker. You will need to attend panel when a match for the child with specific adopters is considered; or when panel is considering the suitability of a prospective adopter. This chapter describes the membership and remit of an adoption panel and describes how you can prepare for attending panel so that it is a constructive experience rather than a daunting one.

Legislation

The composition, terms of reference and duties of panels are laid down in the Adoption Agencies Regulations (AAR) 2005.

Duties of the panel

Adoption panels must consider and make a recommendation about:

- whether the child should be placed for adoption, where there is parental consent to the child being adopted and the agency does not intend to apply for a placement order.

  It must also consider, and may give advice, about

  - proposed contact arrangements

  - an application for a placement order

- whether a prospective adopter is suitable to adopt a child.

  It may also consider and give advice about the number of children, their age range, likely needs and background.

- the termination of approval of a prospective adopter.

- whether the child should be placed for adoption with that particular prospective adopter.

  It must also consider and may give advice about

  - the proposed adoption support services

  - the proposed contact arrangements

  - any restrictions (pre-adoption order) on the birth parent's or the prospective adopter's parental responsibility.

Other duties

Some panels, often called adoption and permanence panels, also consider long-term fostering plans and matches for children, concurrent planning or Fostering for Adoption placements. Some also consider proposed special guardianship arrangements for looked after children. This is not required by regulations but may be part of the agreed decision-making process in your agency.

Who is on an adoption panel?

The agency must maintain a central list of people whom it considers suitable to be members of an adoption panel. There is no limit to the number of people who can be included on the central list. Statutory guidance 1.27 and Annex B, and the Adoption Agencies and Independent Review of Determinations (Amendment) Regulations 2011 state that this 'pool of people with different skills, experience and qualifications allows the most appropriate members to consider individual cases and reduce the likelihood of panel meetings being postponed', including:

The Chair (the central list must include at least one individual with the qualities to chair an adoption panel), independent of the agency, with:

- a sound understanding of the adoption process (or the ability to develop this quickly with appropriate training);
- the authority and competence to chair a panel;
- the ability to analyse and explain complex information;
- the ability to identify key issues, problems and solutions; and
- excellent interpersonal, oral and written communication skills.

The Vice Chair (individuals with the qualities to act as Vice Chair, and with the necessary skills and experience to deputise for the Chair). There is no requirement for the Vice Chair to be independent of the agency, although this is preferable.

Social workers: one or more social workers with at least three years' relevant post-qualifying experience. Relevant experience should be in child care social work, including direct experience in adoption work. These social workers do not need to be employed by the agency.

Agency's medical adviser: where the agency has more than one medical adviser, they may all be included on the central list.

Other persons: these will include individuals who are not employed by the agency and whose appointment would help reflect the independent nature of the panel. Suitable members could include specialists in education, child and adolescent mental health, race and culture, and also those who have personal experience of adoption.

Quorum

The panel can only consider cases if at least five members (six for joint panels) are present. These must include the Chair or Vice Chair and a social worker with at least three years' post-qualifying experience. Where the Vice Chair has to chair the meeting, and is not an independent member, at least one independent member must attend.

Other people who will be present or provide advice to the ADM

Agency adviser to panel

This could be the adoption manager or other senior manager or, increasingly, someone who has this as their sole role. The adviser must be a social worker with at least five years' relevant post-qualifying experience and relevant management experience. AAR 8 sets out their responsibilities and qualifications. They are not a panel member but should attend panel meetings and give such advice to the panel and the ADM as the panel or ADM may request in relation to any case or generally.

One of their key roles is before panel. They have a responsibility, set out in Adoption Guidance 1.32, to 'maintain an overview of the quality of the agency's reports, to both the panel and to the decision-maker, and liaise with team managers to quality assure the child's permanence report, the prospective adopter's report and the adoption placement report. Where there are concerns about a report, the agency adviser and the panel Chair should consider whether it is adequate for submission to the panel. It will be for the agency adviser alone to decide whether the report is adequate for submission to the decision-maker.' This is discussed further in the section later in this chapter, "Preparing for the adoption panel".

Legal adviser

The legal adviser is not usually a panel member. However, they usually attend panel and can provide advice to the ADM. The panel 'must obtain legal advice in relation to the case' when considering adoption as the plan for a child (AAR 18(2)(c)). It is very helpful if the legal adviser is in attendance at panel to give legal advice on the case and to answer questions that panel members may have.

Administrator/minute taker

AAR 5 requires a written record of panel proceedings, its recommendations and the reasons for the recommendations. The administrator or a minute taker prepares minutes.

The administrator is usually also responsible for receiving and sending out papers to panel members and so is an important person for you to liaise with before panel (see "Preparing for the adoption panel").

Observer

There may be an observer at panel, usually not more than one. They must sign a confidentiality statement. They do not speak at panel.

Tenure of panel members

The Regulations (2011) state that 'A person who is included in the central list may at any time ask to be removed from the central list by giving one month's notice in writing. Where the adoption agency is of the opinion that a person included in the central list is unsuitable or unable to remain in the list the agency may remove that person's name from the list by giving them one month's notice in writing with reasons.'

Preparing for the adoption panel

It can be helpful to attend panel as an observer before attending to present a case. The panel administrator or agency adviser usually do the booking for this and would be the people to discuss it with.

You could also ask for any written information about panel members and the panel process that your agency has. Most have a leaflet for social workers on this. If there is nothing in writing the agency adviser should be able to answer any questions and to talk you through the process. (See *Further reading* at the end of this chapter for useful publications.)

The panel administrator will have dates for panels for the next year, including the deadlines for submission of paperwork to him or her for each panel. It is important to liaise with the panel administrator as soon as possible to book a panel slot which will meet with other deadlines you may have, e.g. for court, but which will also give you time to have your reports ready by the panel deadline.

It is important that your manager attends panel with you if at all possible and so you need to check dates with him or her.

The key reports which will be needed by panel or the ADM when it considers adoption as the plan for the child are:

- the child's permanence report – this important report is discussed in Chapter 4;

- the medical adviser will have a copy of the child's health report and information relating to the health of the child's birth parents. These reports are not usually circulated to other panel members but the information should be summarised in the child's permanence report.

There will probably be other reports and assessments that experts may have written about the possibility of birth parents or other relatives caring for the child and that should be shared with the panel. However, it is preferable if you can summarise them in the child's permanence report, although usually the panel must have access to the full report. Sometimes you may think it would be helpful to submit the whole report rather than a summary and you could liaise with the agency adviser about this. You should liaise with the legal adviser about court reports.

Where a case is considered directly by the ADM, you will need to provide the same documentation. Your agency will have its own guidance for managing the process for these cases. The ADM may not refer non-consent cases to panel but may discuss the case with the agency adviser and take medical and legal advice from the medical and legal advisers respectively.

The key documents needed when taking a match to panel are described in Chapter 9, *Finding a family and making a match*.

Timescales

Adoption Guidance 2.2 specifies that:

- the adoption panel should receive all necessary information from the agency within six weeks of the completion of the child's permanence report;

- the adoption panel's recommendation on whether the child should be placed for adoption should be made within two months of a review where adoption has been identified as the permanence plan.

Adoption Guidance 1.56 states that 'the decision-maker must make the decision within seven working days of receipt of the reports referred to in AAR 17.2D or, as applicable, the recommendation and final set of minutes of the adoption panel or independent review panel.'

The Adoption Guidance states that:

The following timescales should generally be adhered to during this part of the adoption process, unless the agency considers that in a particular case complying with a timescale would not be in the child's interests – the paramount consideration must always be the welfare of the child. Where the agency is unable to comply with a timescale or decides not to, it should record the reasons on the child's case record (2.2).

The child's guardian

The panel is required by case law to know the views of the guardian and statutory guidance requires the ADM to also be made aware of them, particularly if they differ from the agency view. CoramBAAF has a form that can be used and included in the CPR.

Sometimes guardians wish to attend panel. This can be arranged by the agency adviser to the panel and you should refer any enquiries from the guardian to the agency adviser. There should be a clear process, agreed with the Chair, for managing attendance. The purpose of attendance is for the guardian to make clear to the panel what his or her views are and to answer any questions. It is not a forum for them to engage in discussion with you about the pros and cons of your possibly different views on the case. You could check with the panel adviser as to how the guardian's attendance and input will be managed, if they wish to attend.

Attending panel

You should be given a time-slot for your case. It is obviously important to be there on time although you do need to be prepared for the possibility of panel running late. It can be difficult to know exactly how long a particular case will take.

It is a good idea to take the child's case file to panel if possible, in case you need to check a piece of information. You should certainly take copies of any reports you have sent to panel as these will be referred to.

You can check beforehand with the agency adviser to panel or the administrator about the panel process. Many panels formulate their questions first and then invite the social worker and manager in. They often ask whether you have any updating information, and then ask their questions. You can give any further relevant information, which you think has been missed, at the end of the questions. The panel will then usually reach its recommendation while you are still in attendance.

Panel members want the same as you do – a good outcome for the child. Provided you have done your work adequately, there should be no surprises in what they ask.

What will the panel and ADM be looking for?

If your child's permanence report (CPR) is up to date and as comprehensive as possible, the panel's and ADM's issues should be addressed. (See Chapter 4 for full information on writing a CPR.) These include:

- the child's current legal status and position regarding any current legal proceedings;
- how and why the child came to the attention of children's services;
- what help the child's parents were given to enable them to provide adequate care;
- whether extended family members have been involved;

- the wishes and feelings of birth parents and others about the plan;

- the child's understanding of what has happened and what is planned and their wishes and feelings about the plan;

- the plan for contact and the wishes and feeling of the child, birth parents and others about this;

- an assessment of the child's development and needs;

- an assessment of the parenting capacity of the birth parents;

- a chronology of the actions and decisions taken by the agency;

- an analysis of the options for the future care of the child, an analysis of the other realistically possible care options that have been considered and why adoption is the preferred plan.

Many, if not most, cases of plans for a child are presented to the ADM during care proceedings. The agency must have a clear care plan for adoption before it refers the case to the ADM. This cannot be conditional on the outcome of any assessments of birth parents or extended family members, or for any other reason. However, it is the agency that must be clear on this. If the guardian or parents' solicitors ask for further assessments that the agency takes the view are unnecessary, then you can still present a clear care plan for adoption to the ADM. You will need to be clear why you think additional assessments are unnecessary. However, the ADM will need to hear about the additional assessments and will then need to come to a view on whether he/she can recommend adoption as the plan.

What can the panel recommend?

The panel can recommend:

- that the child should be placed for adoption;

- that the child should not be placed for adoption;

  or

- can defer making a recommendation because it does not have all the information it requires. If this is the case, it should be specific in listing the information it requires and it should, if possible, set a date for this and for the panel it hopes the case will be re-presented to. It is important that you and your manager are as clear as possible with panel members about what is realistic and about what the barriers, if any, are to the gathering of the information requested. You should ask the panel if you are unclear what it is they are asking for.

What happens next?

The decision

The panel's recommendation and reasons, and the minutes of their discussion, go to the ADM, who should already have all the reports that were sent to the panel. The ADM is a senior manager, often the Director of Children's Services. He or she is required by Adoption Guidance 1.56 to make a decision on whether the child should be placed for adoption within *seven working days* of the adoption panel's recommendation or receipt of the reports in non-consent cases.

The ADM is required to consider the panel minutes but is not, however, obliged to agree with the panel recommendation. If he or she is minded not to agree with it, this must be discussed with another senior person in the agency who is not a panel member and the outcome of this discussion should be recorded on the child's case record.

In non-consent cases, the ADM will not have a recommendation from the panel and will make the decision after considering the reports and taking advice from the agency adviser and medical or legal adviser, as necessary.

Notifying parents

The child's parent or guardian should be informed orally of the agency's decision within *two working days* and written confirmation should be sent to them within *five working days*. You need to liaise with the panel administrator or the ADM about the written confirmation as it is often he or she who sends this. The verbal information is probably best given by you, after discussion with your manager.

Panel minutes

Draft minutes will be produced after the panel, usually checked by the Chair and/or agency adviser and sent to the decision-maker.

The minutes will be formally approved by the panel as quickly as possible (this may be done electronically) and you should then have a copy of the minutes of your case for the child's file. (You may also be sent a copy of the draft minutes before this as a reminder of tasks which may have been identified by panel.)

Courts sometimes ask for a copy of the minutes of a particular case. You should liaise with the administrator and the agency adviser to the panel about arranging for these to be sent. It will need to be made clear whether the minutes are draft or have been formally agreed by the panel.

Feedback after the panel

Many panels have a feedback sheet that they ask presenting social workers to complete after panel. It is important for them to hear your views on the panel process, both before and during the panel. If you are not given a sheet but have comments, you could discuss with your manager and the agency adviser to the panel about how to feed these back.

Some panels also give feedback to workers on their presentation at panel. If this isn't done but you would find it helpful, do discuss this with your manager and the agency adviser.

Fostering for Adoption and concurrent planning

These cases will not come to panel unless parental consent to adoption is given. The Early Permanence statutory guidance sets out the process for deciding that a child should be placed with dually approved carers who would go on to adopt the child if the plan becomes adoption.

FURTHER READING

Lord J and Cullen D (2013) *Effective Adoption Panels*, London: BAAF (new edn forthcoming 2016)

BAAF and Coram (2013) *Fostering for Adoption: Practice guidance*, London: BAAF, available at: www.corambaaf.org.uk/webfm-send/3217

Routes by which a child comes to panel with a proposed adoption plan

5

Looked after children

Child relinquished for adoption by birth parents

Child relinquished for adoption by birth parents	Looked after children
Adoption being requested by birth parents. Other options not appropriate.	Birth parent(s) in contact with LA. May be self-referral or referral by eg. GP, school, health visitor.
Child may be accommodated in foster care.	Assessment of child's needs and whether they are being, or could be, met by the birth family, including extended family.
Statutory counselling of parents about adoption.	Work with family to enable them to parent their child adequately.
Decision to plan for adoption confirmed at review.	Help may include offering respite care or temporary foster care. This could include placement with relatives. → Child remains at or is returned home.
Adoption panel for recommendation that child should be placed for adoption.	Case conference/review decision that child should be removed from home or remain looked after. Parents agree.
Agency decision-maker agrees the plan and parents notified.	Child looked after by LA in foster home or children's home under s.20 Ch Act 1989.
CAFCASS officer witnesses consent to adoption. (Child at least 6 weeks old.) Child under 6 weeks of age can be placed with adopters with written agreement of birth parent(s).	Assessment of child's needs. Further work with family. Permanence plan made by review at 4 months. → Return home or special guardianship or long-term fostering.

Decision to plan for adoption confirmed at review. Child may already be subject to a care order made previously. Parents now agree with adoption plan.

Statutory counselling of parents about adoption. They are still in agreement.

Adoption panel for recommendation that child should be placed for adoption.

Agency decision-maker agrees the plan and parents notified.

Parents agree and sign their consent witnessed by CAFCASS – s.19 ACA 2002.

Adapted from *Effective Adoption Panels* (Lord and Cullen, 2016)

6 Contact

Contact – the legislation

Contact arrangements must be considered carefully at various stages in the adoption process. These are set out in the AAR and in Chapter 7 of the Adoption Guidance. They are described in the various chapters of this guide but are summarised below. The Children and Families Act 2014 introduced a new order which can prohibit contact and can be made when the adoption order is made or at any time after that, but at the time of writing is not referred to in the adoption statutory guidance.

The "welfare checklist" in the Adoption and Children Act 2002 section 1

This is of overarching importance. It must be considered in every decision about adoption made by the agency and by the court. It includes 'The relationship which the child has with relatives, and with any other person ... including the likelihood of any such relationship continuing and the value to the child of its doing so'.

Considering and deciding whether a child should be placed for adoption

- The child must be counselled and his or her wishes and feelings about contact must be ascertained as far as is reasonably practicable (AAR 13).

- The birth parent(s), guardian, or any other person the agency considers relevant, must have their wishes and feelings about contact with the child, should adoption become the plan, ascertained. The counselling for parent(s) and guardians must explain the implications for contact from the point the agency is authorised to place the child for adoption.

- A child's permanence report must be written when adoption is considered the preferred option. It must include the wishes and feelings of the child and of his or her parent(s) or guardian, and any other person the agency considers relevant, about contact after authorisation to place and also after adoption (AAR 17).

  It must also include the agency's views on contact and the arrangements it proposes to make for allowing contact.

- Where the adoption panel considers whether the child should be placed for adoption, it must consider the proposed contact arrangements. It may give advice to the agency about these (AAR 18).

Once the decision is made that the child should be placed for adoption

Once a formal decision has been made, AAR 46 requires the agency to consider what arrangements it should make for allowing any contact, once it is authorised to place the child for adoption.

In deciding on contact, AAR 46.3 requires that:

- the wishes and feelings of the parent or guardian are taken into account – this will include a father without parental responsibility if this is considered appropriate;

- the advice given by the adoption panel (where it has considered the case) should also be taken into account;

- Sections 1(2) and (4) of the Adoption and Children Act are to be considered: s.1(2) provides that the paramount consideration … must be the child's welfare, throughout his or her life. Section 1(4) includes:

  - the child's ascertainable wishes and feelings (considered in the light of the child's age and understanding)

  - the child's particular needs

  - any harm which the child has suffered or is at risk of suffering

  - the relationship the child has with relatives, and with any other person the agency considers relevant and the likelihood and value of this relationship continuing.

Application for a placement order

If an application for a placement order needs to be made, a court report must be written. What should be included in this is set out in Annex B to the Family Procedure (Adoption) Rules. The 2014 version of CoramBAAF's CPR has been designed so that, following the agency decision, it can be used as the Annex B report to accompany the placement order application.

You will be required to record the wishes and feelings about contact of the child and of the parents or guardian, the actual contact with parents and the child's relationship with other relatives. You will also be required to detail the support and advice given to the parents and any services offered or taken up.

Your recommendations must include whether there should be future contact arrangements (or not) and whether a contact order under s.26 or s.51A of the Adoption and Children Act should be made.

Authorisation to place a child for adoption or agreement to place an infant under six weeks old

- Authorisation to place, either by consent or a placement order, or the placing for adoption of a child under six weeks old, means that any existing contact order ceases to have effect.

- AAR 45.2 removes the general duty in the Children Act 1989 to promote contact. Adoption Guidance Chapter 7 states that:

  There should be no general presumption for or against contact (7.1)…Contact arrangements should be focused and shaped around the child's needs. The child's welfare is the paramount consideration at all times and each child's needs for contact should be individually considered (7.8)…Contact arrangements may need to be varied as the child's relationships and needs for contact change over time (7.11).

- AAR 45 removes the general obligation in the 1989 Act to consult with birth parents before making any decision about the child. However, the local authority can still consult and consider the views of parents if it wishes.

6

Section 26 contact

When the court makes a placement order, it must consider actual and proposed contact arrangements, and the views of the parties, and may make a contact order under s.26 of the Adoption and Children Act even if there has been no application for one.

The child, the local authority, parent(s), guardians, relatives, holders of previous child arrangements, contact or residence orders, can apply under s.26 for a contact order. Others, including the child's prospective adopters, can apply for a s.26 contact order with the leave of the court.

Matching and proposing a placement

- When a placement with particular prospective adopters is being considered, the agency must discuss the proposed contact arrangements with them and ascertain their views on these (AAR 31).

- If the agency considers the placement should proceed, it must write an adoption placement report which will include the proposed contact arrangements. The prospective adopter(s) must be given 10 working days to make any observations on these (AAR 31.2).

- The panel that considers the match must consider these contact arrangements and the prospective adopter(s') comments on them. The panel may give advice to the agency on the proposed contact arrangements (AAR 32).

Making a placement

- Once a child has been formally matched for adoption via the panel, the agency is required to prepare a draft adoption placement plan, including contact arrangements, to discuss this with the prospective adopters and then to include contact arrangements in a final adoption placement plan (AAR 35).

Reviews after placement

- Reviews must consider the existing arrangements for contact and whether these should continue or be altered.

Application to court for an adoption order and s.51A contact

- The Annex A court report (see Chapter 14, *Applying for the adoption order*) must include the wishes and feelings of the child in relation to contact (having regard to the child's age and understanding), each parent and guardian's wishes and feelings in relation to contact, the extent of contact with each parent and the nature of the relationship, the child's relationships with other relatives, the likelihood of such relationships continuing and the value to the child of its doing so.

The prospective adopter's wishes and feelings in relation to contact must also be included.

- The report must include the agency's proposals for contact, including options for facilitating or achieving any indirect or direct contact, and the agency's opinion on the likely effect on the security of the placement of any proposed contact.

- Section 46(6) of the Adoption and Children Act requires the court to consider whether there should be arrangements for contact before making an adoption order. It must hear the views of all the parties. There is no "presumption" of contact.

- The Adoption and Children Act 2014 introduced a new s.51A to the ACA 2002. This enables the court, before or after making an adoption order, to consider whether there should be any order made about contact arrangements. The court is able – on its own initiative or following an application from the adoptive parents, the child or anyone who has obtained the court's leave to make an application – to make either a contact order or an order prohibiting contact between the child and a named person or people.

Contact – practice issues

Purpose of contact

As described above, the legislation requires that the child's welfare is paramount. Any contact arrangements must benefit the child and must be geared to meeting the child's needs and not primarily those of the adults involved. Contact may be about maintaining or building a relationship or it may be primarily to keep alive a sense of the child's origins. It may reassure the child about the well-being of relatives or about their continuing care and concern for him or her. The purpose will help determine the sort of contact that is arranged.

The individual child's wishes and feelings, needs and welfare should be at the heart of any plan for contact. What does this particular child need? Who do they want contact with and how feasible is this? Could there be benefits in direct contact for a baby, if the relatives support the adoption and can perhaps, be an additional grandparent or aunt for the child? Is it likely to be helpful for this child to maintain contact with foster carers with whom there is a strong bond?

Crucially, the child's needs are likely to change over time. Contact arrangements made when the child is very young are unlikely to be appropriate when the child is a teenager.

Preparation and support of the child

The child's wishes and feelings about contact must be sought and listened to. Their messages about this are likely to be through their behaviour as well as verbally and these need to be attended to carefully.

You may sometimes need to explain to children why they are not able to have direct contact with people even though they would like to. You may need to go through their life story again to remind them of that person's inability to keep them safe. Siblings should not be expected to keep secrets from each other and so, if there are safety issues for the child being adopted and other siblings are still in the birth family or in direct contact with family members, direct contact may not be possible. You will need to explain this as clearly as possible to the child. If direct contact is to cease, at least for some time, it is important that the child is clear about this. It may be helpful to have a visit that everyone knows is the last one for some time.

Both you and the adopters will need to understand the impact of social media on contact. Research shows that the adopted child is more likely to instigate social media searching or contact than the birth family, often without the knowledge of their adoptive family. Support for the child should be ongoing and reflect his changing needs and curiosity about his birth family and the benefits of supported contact.

Preparation and support of the birth family

As described above, the birth parents, including the birth father without parental responsibility if the agency considers this appropriate, and any other relatives or friends whom the agency considers appropriate, are required by legislation to be consulted about and involved in decisions about contact.

For direct contact to work they must be prepared to be broadly supportive of the adoption placement. If they are very against the plan, it may be hard for them not to be undermining of the placement. This will clearly not be helpful for the child. However, with help and support, birth family members may be able to move on and to accept that the adoption is going to happen and that they still have something positive to give the child, through either direct or indirect contact. Birth parents may oppose the placement order and the adoption order so that the decision is removed from them but it may not mean that they will be unable to co-operate over contact.

Things which may help include:

- attendance at a support group for birth parents – enquire whether your adoption team or regional post-adoption or after adoption centre know of any;

- individual counselling, either through adoption services as above or possibly accessed through the health service via the GP;

- a meeting between the prospective adopters and birth relatives. This can be extremely helpful to both birth relatives and adopters. It makes them real for each other and can be very reassuring. It is likely to make future indirect, as well as any direct, contact easier.

Authorisation to place

The section on legislation makes it clear what a significant stage this is in the process towards adoption. Once you have a placement order (or witnessed consent to placement), there is no longer a presumption of contact or a duty to consult birth parents about every decision.

Even if it may be some time before the child is actually placed for adoption, contact must be looked at afresh and it may be appropriate to start reducing it in preparation for the contact arrangements after placement. It may be that this significant legal step can be used to help birth relatives understand and accept that an adoption really is going to happen. They may be able to consider contact arrangements in a different way now that the main legal process is over.

Preparation and support of the adopters

The adopters' worker will have discussed contact issues at length with them during their assessment. However, when matching is being considered, they need to be prepared for the particular contact arrangements that are being proposed for this individual child. You are required to consult with them about the contact arrangements and to get their views on these. Contact is much more likely to work if adopters have been involved and feel that their views have been listened to and taken into account in the final contact plan. You will need to liaise with the adopters' worker and the family finder about this. Although adopters have the right to apply for a "no contact" order, social media means that direct contact is likely to occur at some point, perhaps initiated by the child. Preparation and support should address issues such as communicative openness and capacity to meet the birth parents, and how they will support the child's changing needs, especially if the child initiates contact.

Written agreements, flexibility and review

As already described, legislation requires that contact arrangements are made before the child is placed for adoption and are set out in the adoption placement plan. It will be important, too, to have a written agreement between the prospective adopters and the birth relatives setting out what each will do. There is a sample adoption agreement in *Ten Top Tips for Managing Contact* (Bond, 2007). The agreement needs to be clear about who will write, when they will write, what people will be called (e.g Mummy Anne rather than just Mummy for the birth mother), whether the agency will check the contents and what support and help they will offer.

Contact arrangements must be formally reviewed during the placement until the child is adopted. There should be some flexibility as it is seen what works and what doesn't, with possible changes to the contact plan discussed and re-negotiated. As explained before, this will need to continue as the child grows up and there should be provision in the adoption support service for a review of arrangements and the drawing up of a new agreement, if necessary, as the child's needs change.

Contact arrangements

Direct contact

If there is to be direct, face-to-face contact, how will this be arranged? It may be that your child's adopters can liaise directly with the adopters of a sibling or with the child's former foster carers or with the child's grandparent. If contact, perhaps with a parent, needs to be set up and even supervised, who will do this once the child is adopted? You will need to ensure that the adoption support worker, if there is one, in your adoption team, is involved from early on and is able and prepared to do what is planned.

Letterbox contact

If contact is to be indirect, by letters exchanged via the agency, is there a scheme for this? Most authorities do have a letterbox scheme, usually run by the adoption support workers. You will probably be involved in explaining the scheme to the birth family members involved and so you need to find out how your agency's scheme is organised. Schemes do vary with some, for example, just sending letters on and others opening and checking them before forwarding them.

The timing of exchanges needs to be carefully considered. It may be appropriate for a birthday and festive greetings card to be exchanged but for the letters with news to be arranged for a different time of year when they won't be just one of many communications. How will the child be involved? Even young children can draw a picture or sign a card. Older children may want to participate more, or less, in writing something.

If photos are sent, is there any danger that these could be used to trace a child? This has happened and there are a number of websites where relatives have posted photos of their children in an effort to locate them. This will need careful consideration in some cases.

It is very important that the contact arrangements for a child are designed to meet his or her individual needs. There is a tendency for letterbox contact, in particular, to be a routine once or twice a year for everyone, but it should not be seen as the easy option: it can have a significant impact on the child and must be handled carefully. Your child may need more frequent letterbox contact with one relative, perhaps a grandparent or sibling, but less or none with another. If it has been impossible to engage a birth parent in discussion about the adoption plan and the contact arrangements, it is probably unrealistic to set up any contact. This can always be re-negotiated in the future, with the agreement of the adopters, and should be discussed with them.

Social media contact

This will be less easy to monitor and it has been found that such contact is often initiated by the child as they grow older. Whilst you need to give it some thought and ensure as far as you can that birth relatives and the child will not try to use this form of contact outside agreed contact arrangements, the adoptive family will need to give continued thought to this. You and they may find some of the publications at the end of this section helpful. They should also have addressed this with their social worker in their own training and assessment. You will need to involve the child as well as their birth relatives in a discussion about this. The child needs to know what to do if he or she receives unsolicited social media contact requests, emails, phone calls or texts.

A spirit of openness

This is how one adopter approached parenting her adopted daughter in a situation where no member of her daughter's birth family wanted any contact at all. She used the information that she had about them to talk about them and to keep them "alive", to some extent, for her daughter. This "communicative openness" has been shown to be more helpful for the child than a grudging agreement to more direct contact.

In all situations, but particularly in ones where there may be no contact, the child's life story book, and any other information, mementoes or photos that you have been able to gather, will be vitally important.

Support

You will be involved, with the adopters' social worker and, probably, the adoption support worker, in supporting the child, their birth relatives and their adoptive parents with contact arrangements up to the point of the adoption order. You will need to be clear what the support arrangements will be after that and to ensure that these are clearly set up with adoption support services either in your agency or from an independent agency. The adoption team should be able to advise on this.

A flowchart follows, devised from a summary of research findings, and may be helpful in managing contact now or in the future.

FURTHER READING

Adams P (2012) *Planning for Contact in Permanent Placements*, London: BAAF

Argent H (ed) (1995) *See You Soon: Contact with children looked after by local authorities*, London: BAAF, Chapter 6, Smith G, 'Do children have a right to leave their pasts behind them? Contact with children who have been abused', pp 85–99

Argent H (ed) (2002) *Staying Connected: Managing contact in adoption*, London: BAAF

Bond H (2007) *Ten Top Tips for Managing Contact*, London: BAAF

Fursland E (2013) *Facing up to Facebook: A survival guide for adoptive families*, London: BAAF

Macaskill C (2002) *Safe Contact: Children in permanent placement and contact with their birth relatives*, London: Russell House Publishing

Neil E and Howe D (eds) (2004) *Contact in Adoption and Permanent Foster Care*, London: BAAF

Neil E, Beek M and Ward E (2015) *Contact after Adoption: A longitudinal study of post-adoption contact arrangements*, London: CoramBAAF

BOOKS FOR USE WITH CHILDREN

Argent H (2004) *What is Contact? A guide for children*, London: BAAF

Foxon J (2003) *Nutmeg Gets a Letter*, London: BAAF

Decision making and contact in permanent placement

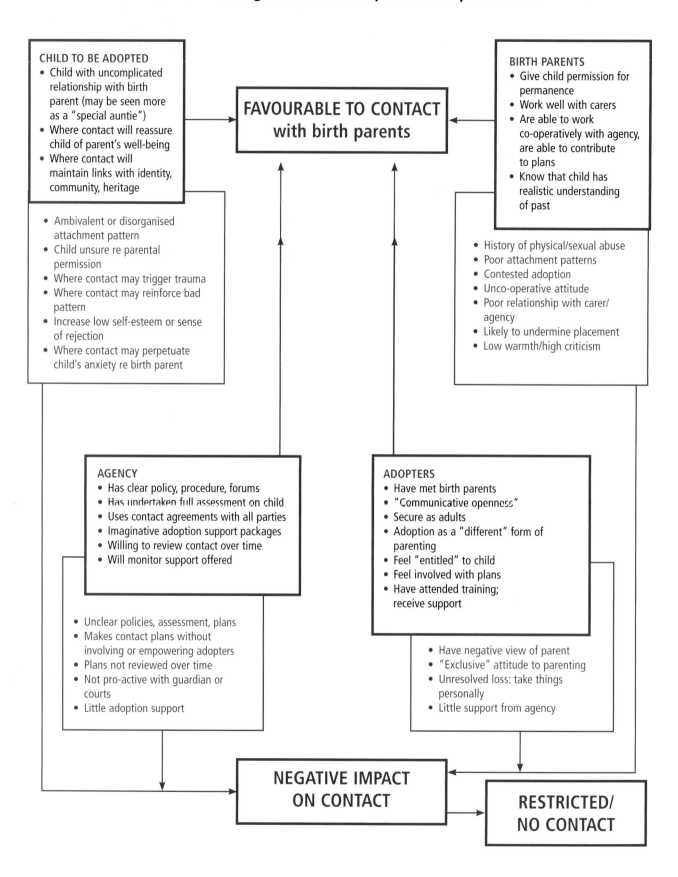

CHILD TO BE ADOPTED
- Child with uncomplicated relationship with birth parent (may be seen more as a "special auntie")
- Where contact will reassure child of parent's well-being
- Where contact will maintain links with identity, community, heritage

FAVOURABLE TO CONTACT with birth parents

BIRTH PARENTS
- Give child permission for permanence
- Work well with carers
- Are able to work co-operatively with agency, are able to contribute to plans
- Know that child has realistic understanding of past

- Ambivalent or disorganised attachment pattern
- Child unsure re parental permission
- Where contact may trigger trauma
- Where contact may reinforce bad pattern
- Increase low self-esteem or sense of rejection
- Where contact may perpetuate child's anxiety re birth parent

- History of physical/sexual abuse
- Poor attachment patterns
- Contested adoption
- Unco-operative attitude
- Poor relationship with carer/agency
- Likely to undermine placement
- Low warmth/high criticism

AGENCY
- Has clear policy, procedure, forums
- Has undertaken full assessment on child
- Uses contact agreements with all parties
- Imaginative adoption support packages
- Willing to review contact over time
- Will monitor support offered

ADOPTERS
- Have met birth parents
- "Communicative openness"
- Secure as adults
- Adoption as a "different" form of parenting
- Feel "entitled" to child
- Feel involved with plans
- Have attended training; receive support

- Unclear policies, assessment, plans
- Makes contact plans without involving or empowering adopters
- Plans not reviewed over time
- Not pro-active with guardian or courts
- Little adoption support

- Have negative view of parent
- "Exclusive" attitude to parenting
- Unresolved loss: take things personally
- Little support from agency

NEGATIVE IMPACT ON CONTACT

RESTRICTED/ NO CONTACT

Prepared by Fran Moffat, BAAF, 2006

Note: the diagram refers to contact with birth parents but can also be used for contact with other birth relatives, including siblings. The adopters or other persons listed in s.51A of the Adoption and Children Act 2014 may apply for an order requiring or prohibiting contact.

7 Adoption support services

Support – the legislation

The Adoption Agencies Regulations (AAR) set out the requirements for considering the provision of adoption support while the child is still looked after. The Adoption Support Services Regulations 2005 (ASR) set out the range of services which can be provided, the people eligible to receive them, and the process for assessing needs and providing services.

In addition, the school admissions code has been amended so that children adopted from care have priority access for school places. They are also eligible for the pupil premium. Adoption support entitlements are set out in the Adoption Passport, which can be accessed on the First4Adoption website (www.first4adoption.org.uk). It is a rapidly changing area.

The Adoption Support Fund (ASF), which covers the provision of therapeutic interventions, was piloted in 2014 and launched nationally in May 2015. The Government plans to increase the fund every year during the current Parliament. Since April 2016, support has been extended to adopted young people up to age 21; extended to special guardians who care for children previously looked after; and will be accessible for children adopted from other countries via intercountry adoption.

Support needs should be considered carefully at various stages in the adoption process. These are described in the various chapters of this guide but are summarised below.

When considering the child's needs and whether they should be placed for adoption

At this stage it is already likely to be clear for some children at least that there will be support needs in relation to their health, education, identity needs, therapeutic needs or need for contact with birth family members. It is likely to be clear too what the support needs of birth family members may be in relation to contact. It will be important to start thinking about these needs at this relatively early stage as they will inform later family finding.

Making a family-finding plan

The child's likely need for support after placement for adoption across a range of factors as described above will need to be considered carefully at this stage. It will be relevant for the sort of adoptive family that is sought.

Considering possible families

When considering possible adoptive families for the child, his or her need for support in relation to identity needs, behaviour and therapeutic needs, health, education, contact – in fact, the whole list of needs and factors detailed in Chapter 9, *Finding a family and making a match* – should be carefully considered. How will each family be able to meet these needs and what additional support from the agency will they require?

At this point, too, the family's own identified needs for support, which should have been flagged up in their assessment, will have to be considered.

Matching

When a specific chosen family is being considered, AAR 31 requires that an assessment of the needs of the child and those of the prospective adopter and any children of the prospective adopter for adoption support services is carried out. (This is described in more detail later in this chapter.) AAR 31 also requires that an Adoption Placement Report (APR) is written detailing, among other things, the 'proposals for the provision of adoption support services for the adoptive family'. These should be discussed and agreed with the family before being put in the draft APR (CoramBAAF's APR includes an Adoption Support Plan that can be updated and used for the APP and ongoing reviews). The prospective adopters then have 10 days to comment on the report, including the support proposals, before it is finalised for the panel. The adopter's comments should go to the panel.

The adopters should be made aware of the support that is available to all adopted children, such as the Pupil Premium, Early Years Pupil Premium, priority access for school places, free early education and childcare, as well as the support that could be made available through the Adoption Support Fund.

Panel

The adoption panel that considers the match is required by AAR 32 to consider the proposals for the provision of adoption support and the prospective adopter's observations and may give advice on them. In extreme cases, if a panel considers that a match is not viable with the level of support that is being proposed, or if the prospective adopter is unhappy about any of the proposed arrangements for support, it could defer making a recommendation until more work has been done on the support proposals. The proposals at this stage should be as clear and concrete as possible. If financial support is proposed, for instance, the financial assessment should have been done so that it is clear what is being offered and the prospective adopters can comment on this.

Adoption placement plan

Once a decision has been made on the match, an adoption placement plan (APP) must be drafted and discussed with the prospective adopters. It must include 'where the local authority has decided to provide adoption support services for the adoptive family, how these will be provided and by whom'. This should include consideration of an application to the Adoption Support Fund (ASF), as this can be made whilst the child is placed for adoption, to come into effect as soon as the adoption order is made. The adopters must be given the Adoption Passport. The final, agreed APP must be really clear and detailed about the support services that will be provided, and if/when an application to the ASF will be made.

Reviews after placement

These must take place 28 days after placement, then at three months, then at six months between placement and adoption order and the arrangements for the provision of adoption support services and 'whether there should be any re-assessment of the need for those services' must be considered at each review. It could well be that the need for extra or different adoption support emerges now that the child is actually in placement, and the need for an application to the ASF may also be identified. It is important that any support needs or services agreed are reviewed and, if appropriate, revised to reflect new information as the child settles into the placement. This may include considering the funding of services through the Adoption Support Fund (ASF) where the needs and services fall within the scope of the Fund.

Court report

The Annex A report written for the adoption order must detail the support being offered at the time and in the future and, if no support is being provided, the reasons why must be given.

After adoption

The Adoption and Children Act 2002, Section 4 stipulates that a local authority must, at the request of an eligible person, assess that person's needs for adoption support services. For the three years following the making of the adoption order, the local authority that placed the child must carry out that assessment. After three years, the local authority in whose area the family lives has the responsibility to carry out that assessment. The exception to this time limit is where the placing local authority agreed to provide financial support before the adoption order was made. In these circumstances, the placing local authority continue to hold that responsibility (Regulation 7, ASSR 2005).

Assessment method

Adoption Guidance 9.45 suggest that the *Framework for the Assessment of Children in Need and their Families* (Department of Health, 2000) is taken as a basis for a support assessment. In relation to the assessment which takes place at the matching stage, it may also be helpful to use the factors involved in matching described in Chapter 9, *Finding a family and making a match*. The needs of the child and new family for support in relation to each of these factors can then be considered. There may well need to be liaison and consultation with health and education authorities and with CAMHS.

You are likely only to be involved in the assessment at the matching stage. This needs to follow the process set out in the ASR and Adoption Guidance. It differs slightly from that used when assessments are done late in the process and after an adoption order, as described below.

Adoption support plan

ASR 16 requires a plan to be prepared, detailing the services to be provided if they are more than advice or information or a one-off service. At the matching stage, the support plan will be part of the adoption placement plan. Adoption Guidance 9.53 specifies that the plan should set out the services to be provided, the objectives and criteria for evaluating success, timescales for provision, procedures for review and the name of the person nominated to monitor the provision of the services in the plan.

The person who has been assessed must be given notice of the outcome, including:

> *a statement as to the person's needs for adoption support services;*
>
> *where the assessment relates to his or her need for financial support, the basis upon which financial support is determined;*
>
> *whether the local authority proposes to provide him or her with adoption support services;*
>
> *the services (if any) that are proposed to be provided;*
>
> *if financial support is to be paid to him or her, the proposed amount that would be payable; and*
>
> *any conditions attached to the payment (Adoption Guidance 9.55).*

They should also be sent a draft of the plan and given a period to comment on this. Adoption Guidance 9.56 suggests 28 days. However, when the assessment is at the matching stage, prospective adopters are allowed 10 days to consider the adoption placement report, which includes the support proposals. You should make sure that they are aware of the support available (see the Adoption Passport at www.first4adoption.org.uk) and that they can return at a later date for an assessment for adoption support.

After considering any representations, a decision must be made on what services will be provided. If financial support is to be given, the prospective adopters must be told the following:

- how the amount of financial support was worked out;
- the amount;
- the frequency of payment;
- the period for which it will be paid.

Financial support

This can be paid to an adoptive parent, as specified in ASR 8:

> a) *where it is necessary to ensure that the adoptive parent can look after the child;*
>
> b) *where the child needs special care which requires greater expenditure of resources by reason of illness, disability, emotional or behavioural difficulties, or the continuing consequences of past abuse or neglect;*
>
> c) *where it is necessary for the local authority to make any special arrangements to facilitate the placement or the adoption by reason of –*
>
>> (i) *the age or ethnic origin of the child, or*
>>
>> (ii) *the desirability of the child being placed with the same adoptive parent as his brother or sister (whether of full or half-blood) or with a child with whom he previously shared a home*
>
> d) *where such support is to meet recurring costs in respect of travel for the purpose of visits between the child and a related person.*

There are certain conditions.

- A means test must usually be done. The format used varies from agency to agency. Your adoption team should be familiar with the one used in your agency. However, Adoption Guidance 9.35 states that the local authority *may disregard means* when considering providing financial support for:

    - a "settling in" grant

    - recurring costs in respect of travel for the child to visit a relative, for example, a sibling

    - any special arrangements or special care referred to in ASR 8(2)(b) and (c) (see earlier in this section) in relation to an agency adoptive child – so local authorities can guarantee a financial package for a particular child who may be difficult to place to facilitate their adoption

    - remuneration to ex-foster carers – so that local authorities can maintain the amount paid to a foster carer who has gone on to adopt for the duration of the transitional period (two years unless the local authority considers the case to be exceptional).

- The local authority *must* disregard means when considering payment for:

    - legal costs, including court fees, in respect of an adoption order application for an agency adoptive child

    - payments to facilitate the introduction of a child to prospective adopters.

There must be an annual review of means when there has been a means test. This is usually a paper exercise.

Any allowance will cease when the child starts work, becomes eligible for benefits in his or her own right or at 18, unless he or she is still in full-time education or training, in which case it may continue until that course or training ends.

Former foster carers and financial support

When foster carers are adopting a child whom they have fostered, the local authority has discretion to pay them the fostering allowance plus any fee they were getting. The fee or remuneration element will usually cease to be paid from two years after the adoption order 'unless the local authority considers its continuation to be necessary having regard to the exceptional needs of the child or any other exceptional circumstances' (ASR 9).

Where the child has been placed in a Fostering for Adoption or concurrent planning placement under s.22C (9A) of the Children Act 1989, the carers are entitled to the foster carer allowance until (and if) the child becomes placed for adoption.

Practice points

The following practice points may be helpful to consider.

A team approach

Although you are likely to know the child better than other workers, the adoptive family's worker is likely to know them best. Many local authorities now have an adoption support worker or team and they, and the family's worker (who may be from a different agency), are likely to be more knowledgeable and experienced about what works in adoption support that you are. An Adoption Support Services Adviser (ASSA) also has to be appointed in each local authority. He or she may be an adoption support worker or manager or may be a more senior manager. This person's role is to be a central point of advice and information on adoption support services, on how assessments for support should be carried out and support plans made, and on what range of services are available, including how to access the ASF to pay for adoption support services. It will be important to find out who this person is in your authority.

It is really important that you liaise closely with these other workers and that there is a joint approach to the assessment for and provision of services. The adoption workers may well take the lead in this but it is important that you are involved. The adoptive parents may also have a view on support needed, and the provider.

You should also consider what support should be offered to the birth family, as this may help them come to terms with the adoption.

Timing

As described earlier, thinking about likely support needs should begin early on, during the assessment of the child and the assessment of the prospective adopters. If this work has been done, the assessment of the support needs of the new family of child and prospective adopter should be easier to do.

Tailor-made plans

Support can only be as good as it feels, and the same package of support will feel different to every child and family. And if it feels good enough at one stage, it may not feel as good at another. (Argent, 2006)

It is important that the support plan for each child and prospective adopter is designed to meet their particular needs and is, as far as possible, what they want and feel comfortable with.

Some adopters will want to do more for themselves than others and may have more support resources available from family and friends than others. Other adopters will need a robust support package to enable them to manage.

It is important that both the prospective adopters and you understand that adoption requires a particular kind of parenting, and that support is likely to be needed because of the child's past experiences and trauma. Adopters should be encouraged to recognise this and not made to feel that needing support is some kind of failure.

What sorts of support can be offered?

Examples of the sorts of support that families may find helpful include the following.

- Training offered to a group of adopters by the local authority on talking about adoption to their child.

- Regular meetings with other adopters arranged by the local authority, voluntary adoption agency or adoption support agency.

- Assistance to fast-track a referral to CAMHS for a consultation and a programme of work with the child and adopters.

- A meeting with the agency medical adviser after placement to discuss the implications of the birth family health history again.

- Facilitation of meetings with birth relatives.

- Support and help to a birth parent to enable him or her to write more constructive and helpful letters to the child.

- Advice from a welfare rights worker on additional benefits which could be claimed for a disabled child.

- Helping adopters to go through the child's life story book again, and the gathering of some additional information if requested.

- Therapeutic interventions such as Theraplay™ or therapeutic parenting to help with behavioural and attachment issues.

- Respite care.

- Financial support.

- How to make an application to the ASF.

Adoption support services that a local authority must have available

The services which must be available for children who have been placed for adoption by an adoption agency and for their families are listed below. The table indicates the services for which individuals are entitled to be assessed. This is likely to be relevant after children are placed and even adopted but may be helpful for you to know about.

The 'services to ensure the continuation of the adoptive relationship' include training for the adopters and also the provision of respite care.

FURTHER READING

Argent H (2003) *Models of Adoption Support: What works and what doesn't*, London: BAAF

Argent H (2006) *Ten Top Tips on Placing Children*, London: BAAF

First4Adoption (2014) *The Adoption Passport: A support guide for adopters*, available at: www.first4adoption.org.uk/wp-content/uploads/2014/07/The-Adoption-Passport.pdf

First4Adoption (2015) *Adoption Support Fund*, available at: www.first4adoption.org.uk/being-an-adoptive-parent/adoption-support/adoption-support-fund/

Kaniuk J and Fursland E (2009) *Ten Top Tips for Supporting Adopters*, London: BAAF

Sunderland M (2007) *What Every Parent Needs to Know: The incredible effects of love, nurture and play on your child's development*, London: DK Publishing

BOOKS FOR USE WITH CHILDREN

Foxon J (2004) *Nutmeg Gets a Little Help*, London: BAAF

Person being assessed	Services for which they are entitled to be assessed						
	Services to enable discussion of matters relating to adoption	Assistance in relation to arrangements for contact	Therapeutic services	Services to ensure the continuation of adoptive relationship	Services to assist in cases of disruption	Counselling advice and information	Financial support
Agency adoptive child	●	●	●	●	●	●	
Adoptive parent of an agency adoptive child	●	●		●	●	●	●
Child of adoptive parent				●	●	●	
Birth parents or guardians of an agency adoptive child	●	●				●	
A relative (or someone with whom the local authority considers the child to have a beneficial relationship) of agency adopted child		●				●	
Intercountry adopted child			●	●	●	●	
Intercountry adoptive parent				●	●	●	
Birth sibling of an adopted child		●				●	
Non-agency adopted children, their parents and guardians						●	
Prospective adopters						●	
Adopted adults, their parent, birth parent and former guardians						●	
A relative (or someone with whom the local authority considers the child to have a beneficial relationship) of a non-agency adopted child						●	

(Taken from Department for Education (2013) *Statutory Guidance on Adoption*, page 166, para 9.8)

Authorisation to place a child for adoption – placement orders and consent

Requirement to have authority to place a child for adoption – Adoption and Children Act, s.18

An adoption agency is authorised to place a child for adoption if it has:

- a placement order; or

- consent under s.19 of the Adoption and Children Act from the parent(s) or guardian.

  It can also place a child for adoption if it has:

- written agreement from the parent(s) for the placement of an infant under six weeks old;

- a freeing order (these can no longer be applied for, but existing orders remain in force) (see Glossary).

  Placements made in the last two ways do not have all the consequences given by authority to place. (Chapter 12 discusses the placement of relinquished infants.)

Placement order

A placement order is an order made by the court authorising a local authority to place a child for adoption with any prospective adopters who may be chosen by the authority (Adoption and Children Act 2002, s.21).

It continues in force until it is revoked, an adoption order is made, the child marries, or forms a civil partnership, or reaches the age of 18.

The court may not make a placement order unless:

- the child is already subject to a care order;

- the grounds for the making of a care order are met; or

- the child has no parent or guardian.

  The court may only make a placement order if it is satisfied that:

- the parent(s) have consented to the child being placed for adoption; or

- their consent should be dispensed with.

Dispensing with parental consent to the making of a placement order

The court may dispense with the consent of a parent or guardian to the making of a placement order on the grounds that:

- the parent cannot be found;

- the parent is incapable of consenting; or
- the welfare of the child requires their consent to be dispensed with.

A placement order extinguishes any existing s.8 order, such as a child arrangements order, residence order, contact order and any supervision order. No s.51A orders may be applied for, except where, at the final adoption order hearing, leave has been given to oppose the making of the adoption order. A child arrangements order or special guardianship order may then be applied for. A s.51A contact order may also be made alongside or after the adoption order.

Children already on care orders

When a child is already on a care order, the local authority can choose whether to place for adoption, with the consent of the parents, if they will give this, or to apply for a placement order. The former is easier in some ways but, if there is any possibility of the consent being withdrawn, it may be safer to apply for a placement order.

Applying for a placement order

Only local authorities may apply for placement orders. The decision-maker must make the decision that the child should be placed for adoption before the local authority can apply for a placement order.

Provided this has been done, the placement order application can be made concurrently with a care order application. The court can make a placement order as the sole order. However, if it makes a care order followed by a placement order, the care order is suspended. It will be re-activated should the placement order be revoked at any point. This will thus provide some protection for the child. Placement order applications are not subject to the 26-week requirement but are usually heard concurrently with the care order application which is subject to that requirement.

Placement order report

The Family Procedure (Adoption) Rules 2005 specify that a report to the court must be made in an application for a placement order. Annex B of the Practice Direction to these Rules sets out what needs to be covered in the placement order application. Consult with your legal department about this.

Revocation of placement orders

Placement orders can be revoked on the application of:

- the local authority;
- the child;
- anyone else, with the leave of the court. The court cannot give leave unless it is satisfied that there has been a change in circumstances since the order was made. The application can only be made, by anyone other than the child or the local authority, if the child has not yet been placed with prospective adopters. If the child has been placed, the birth parent(s) will need to wait until an application is made for an adoption order and can then apply for leave to oppose

it (see Chapter 14, *Applying for the adoption order*, for more information on this). However, challenges to care, placement and adoption orders are increasingly being allowed.

Case law, reported in *Adoption & Fostering*, Volume 31:4 (2007), states that leave for such an application should not be given, even if there has been a change of circumstances since the placement order was made, unless there is a real prospect of success.

Consent to the placement of a child for adoption

Section 19 of the Adoption and Children Act provides for parents or guardians to give their consent to their child being placed for adoption.

A birth mother cannot give formal consent until the child is six weeks old. (However, a child under this age can be placed for adoption, see Chapter 12, *Placing a relinquished infant for adoption*.)

The consent can be specific to placement with particular adopters, or for placement with any adopters chosen by the agency.

At the same time as giving this consent, or subsequently, formal consent may also be given under s.20 to the making of an adoption order. This may be in relation to any adopters chosen by the agency or to adopters specified in the consent.

If they give consent under s.20, the parent or guardian may also give written notice that they do not wish to be notified of the subsequent application for an adoption order. If they do not do this, the court will notify them of the application for an adoption order.

It is important that you offer counselling to the parent(s) and guardian(s) about the adoption plan and about the implications of them giving consent. For more information on this, see the later section on withdrawal of consent and also the section on the implications of authorisation to place a child for adoption.

Timing of consent

The birth mother cannot give formal consent to the adoption until the child is six weeks old. However, she may agree to the child being placed with prospective adopters. Thereafter, it may be best if consent is given formally after the adoption panel has recommended that the child should be placed for adoption and the agency has decided on this as the plan. However, this is not a requirement and in some situations, for instance, if the birth mother disappears, or to avoid delay in going to panel, it could be appropriate to get formal consent before the panel meets. See Adoption Statutory Guidance 2.9–2.94.

Formal witnessing of consent when a child who is not in care proceedings is relinquished for adoption

This must be done by a CAFCASS officer if the parent is in England or Wales. There is a helpful protocol for this process that has been agreed between CAFCASS and the Association of Directors of Children's Services (ADCS). It includes detailed information on the process, standard letters for making the referral to CAFCASS and a pro-forma for the information that you need to provide to CAFCASS under Schedule 2 of the AAR. The protocol can be found on the CAFCASS website at *www.cafcass.gov.uk/publications/policies.aspx*.

Consent in care proceedings

When a case is in care proceedings but the birth parent(s) decide to consent to adoption, the local authority has a choice.

- It can proceed with the care proceedings and apply for a placement order, as described in the section on placement orders. This might be a safer option, unless you are very confident that the parent(s) will not subsequently change their minds.

- It can withdraw the care proceedings, with the leave of the court, and obtain the consent of the parent(s) under s.19.

Parents or guardians living abroad

Where the parents or guardians are outside England and Wales, their consent should be witnessed by a person authorised in that country for this purpose. A CAFCASS officer is not appointed to check or witness their consent.

Father who acquires parental responsibility

When a child has been placed for adoption with the consent of the mother under s.19 and the father then acquires parental responsibility, he is deemed also to have given consent (Adoption and Children Act s.52(9) and (10)).

Withdrawal of consent

The child's parents or guardian can withdraw their consent in writing to the child's placement for adoption at any time until the prospective adopters apply for an adoption order. The child must be returned by the agency to the parents unless it is decided to apply for a placement order (see below).

- If the consent is withdrawn before the child is placed for adoption, the child must be returned to the birth parent within seven days (Adoption and Children Act s.31).

- If the consent is withdrawn after the child has been placed for adoption with prospective adopters but before they have applied to court, the agency must require the prospective adopters to return the child to the adoption agency within 14 days and the agency must immediately return the child to the parent(s) (Adoption and Children Act s.32).

- If consent is withdrawn before an application has been made to court for an adoption order and the local authority considers that the child should still be placed for adoption, it can, if there are grounds, apply for a placement order. An application for a placement order would prevent the child's removal until the court has decided whether or not to make a placement order.

In each of these situations you would need to make immediate contact with your legal department. AAR 38.2 requires the authority, once it has received written notification of withdrawal of consent, to review immediately its decision to place the child for adoption. If it is decided that the child should still be placed for adoption, and if there is legal advice that the prerequisite grounds for making a care order are met, a placement order can be applied for, as described above. If this is the decision, you are required to notify the parent or guardian, a father without parental responsibility if this is considered appropriate, and the prospective adopters, if the child is placed for adoption.

If consent is withdrawn after the prospective adopters have applied to court for an adoption order, the child cannot be removed from the adopters' care and the birth parent may only oppose the final adoption order with the leave of the court, and the court may only grant leave if it is satisfied that there has been a change of circumstances since the parents gave their consent to placement (see Chapter 14, *Applying for the adoption order*, for more information).

Parents in this situation will need to seek legal advice.

Consequences of authority to place a child for adoption

This is a very significant stage in the process towards adoption. Authority to place has an immediate effect on:

- duty to consult parents;
- parental responsibility;
- removal from placement;
- contact;
- applying for other orders;
- opposing an adoption order;
- reviews.

These are discussed in turn.

Duty to consult parents

AAR 45 applies when an agency is authorised to place a child for adoption or has placed a child of less than six weeks old for adoption. It modifies the Children Act 1989 and:

- removes the general obligation in the 1989 Act to ascertain and to consider the wishes and feelings of the child's parents before making any decision about the child;

- requires the local authority to ascertain and to consider the wishes and feelings of prospective adopters with whom a child has been placed before making any decision about the child;

- the authority is still required to ascertain and to consider the wishes and feelings of the child and 'any other person the authority considers relevant'.

Parental responsibility

The agency acquires parental responsibility for the child once it is authorised to place the child for adoption. This is the case even where the child is accommodated. However, it will only acquire parental responsibility for a child placed under the age of six weeks once formal consent under s.19 has been obtained, after the child is six weeks old. The birth parent(s) retain parental responsibility (they only lose it on the making of an adoption order) but once it has authority to place for adoption, the agency can restrict the parent(s)' exercise of their parental responsibility. The prospective adopters will acquire parental responsibility once the child is placed for adoption although the agency can restrict their exercise of it. (They will not acquire parental responsibility until the child is adopted if the placement was made by virtue of a freeing order.)

The child cannot be known by a new surname or removed from the UK (for more than a month) except with the written consent of each parent or guardian or the leave of the court.

Removal from placement

No one other than the local authority may remove a child from a placement whether or not the child is yet placed for adoption and even if the child is placed with s.19 consent or with the agreement of the parents if the child is under six weeks old. However, as described above, the Act requires a child placed with consent to be returned to their parents unless the local authority decides to apply for a placement order or the adopters have applied to court for an adoption order.

Section 31 requires the local authority to return the child to the parents within seven days of the request if the child has not been placed for adoption; s.32 gives the adopters 14 days to return the child if he or she has been placed for adoption.

Contact

AAR 45.2 removes the general duty in the Children Act 1989 to promote contact, once the agency is authorised to place the child for adoption. Adoption Guidance 7.1 states that:

> …the intention [of an adoptive placement] is that the child should become part of another family. Therefore, where the agency is authorised to place the child for adoption, there should be no general presumption for or against contact…Contact arrangements should be focused and shaped around the child's needs.

When the agency is authorised to place a child for adoption, any existing 1989 Act contact order ceases to have effect.

However, an application for a contact order under s.26 of the Adoption and Children Act can be made. (There is further discussion of contact in Chapter 6, *Contact*.) Once the court is making or has made an adoption order, an order permitting or prohibiting contact can be made under s.51A of the Children and Adoption Act 2014.

Applying for other orders

Where there is a placement order, parents cannot apply for any s.8 order under the 1989 Children Act. Parents or guardians who have consented cannot apply for a child arrangements order or special guardianship order. Child arrangements orders or special guardianship orders may only be applied for at the adoption hearing stage, if leave to oppose the adoption order has been given.

Reviews

Statutory reviews of looked after children are covered by the Review of Children's Cases Regulations 1991 and the Review of Children's Cases (Amendment) (England) Regulations 2004 up to the point when a local authority is authorised to place a child for adoption. From that point, the requirement for reviews is covered by AAR 36. (The role of the independent reviewing officer (IRO) is described in Chapter 1, *Making a permanence plan*.) This regulation requires that, in the period before a child is placed for adoption, reviews must be held –

- not more than three months after the date on which the agency first has authority to place; and

- thereafter not more than six months after the date of the previous review until the child is placed for adoption.

When carrying out a review, the agency is required by AAR 36 to ascertain the views of:

- the child, having regard to his or her age or understanding; and

- any other person the agency considers relevant.

This would include the child's parent or guardian where the agency considers it appropriate. There is no longer a legal requirement to get their views and to involve them in the review, although it may well be appropriate to do this in the period before the child is placed for adoption.

Others whose views could usefully be gathered would be the child's current carer, a health visitor, therapist or teacher.

AAR 36.6 sets out the matters which should be considered at the review, in the period before the child is placed for adoption.

These are:

- whether the adoption agency remains satisfied that the child should be placed for adoption;

- the child's needs, welfare and development, and whether any changes need to be made to meet his or her needs or assist his or her development;

- the existing arrangements for contact, and whether they should continue or be altered;

- in consultation with the appropriate agencies, the arrangements for assessing and meeting the child's health care and educational needs;

- the frequency of reviews (subject to the minimum requirement).

AAR 36.7 further requires that:

- where the child is subject to a placement order and has not been placed for adoption at the time of the first six months review, the local authority must at that review:

  - establish why the child has not been placed for adoption and consider what further steps the authority should take in relation to the placement of the child for adoption, and

  - consider whether it remains satisfied that the child should be placed for adoption.

Where it is reasonably practicable, the child and 'any other person whom the agency considers relevant' must be notified of the outcome of the review and any decisions taken. "Any other person" could include the birth parents or other relatives.

A record must be placed on the child's case record of any visits, meetings or decisions made in relation to or at the review.

FURTHER READING

Conroy Harris A (2014) *Ten Top Tips on Going to Court*, London: BAAF

Cullen D and Conroy Harris A (2014) *Child Care Law: A summary of the law in England and Wales*, London: BAAF

Smith F, Stewart R and Conroy Harris A (2013) *Adoption Now: Law, regulations, guidance and standards (England)*, London: BAAF

9 Finding a family and making a match

Timescales

Research is clear that delay in placing a child with his or her permanent family is detrimental to the child's development. Research also shows that, whilst relatively few adoptions disrupt, the age of a child at placement is the single most significant factor:

> Children who were older at entry to care, who had had more moves whilst looked after, and who had waited longer to be placed with their adoptive families were more likely to disrupt. Three-quarters of children who experienced a disruption were more than four years old at placement with their adoptive family. (Selwyn et al, 2015, p338)

It is therefore essential that family finding starts as early as possible and that there are no unnecessary barriers to a good placement.

Adoption Guidance 4.2 specifies the following.

- A proposed placement with a suitable prospective adopter should be identified and approved by the panel within six months of the agency deciding that the child should be placed for adoption.

- Where a birth parent has requested that a child aged under six months be placed for adoption, a proposed placement with a suitable prospective adopter should be identified and approved by the panel within three months of the agency deciding that the child should be placed for adoption.

The Guidance further states that:

> The timescales should be adhered to during this part of the adoption process, unless the adoption agency considers that in a particular case complying with a timescale would not be in the child's interests – the paramount consideration must always be the welfare of the child. Where the agency is unable to comply with a timescale or decides not to, it should record the reasons on the child's case record (4.1).

It also specifies that family finding should begin prior to the ADM decision and the making of the placement order although, where parental consent is not expected and there is doubt as to whether a placement order will be made, it may not be appropriate to make more than general enquires about the suitability of prospective adopters (4.3).

National Minimum Standards for Adoption

National Minimum Standard (NMS) 13 is about matching and placing the child with prospective adopters who can meet most of their assessed needs. It aims to ensure that:

> Children benefit from stable placements and are matched and placed with prospective adopters who can meet most, if not all, of their assessed needs.

Children feel loved, safe and secure with their prospective adoptive parents with whom they were originally placed; and these children were placed within the timeframe set out in the adoption scorecard indicators A1 (average time between a child entering care and moving in with his or her adoptive family, for children who have been adopted) and A2 (average time between a local authority receiving court authority to place a child and the local authority deciding on a match with an adoptive family).

NMS 13.1 requires that the child's details are referred to the Adoption Register when no locally identified match is being actively pursued at the latest by three months after the ADM has decided that the child should be placed for adoption.

No match will be "perfect" and you will need to weigh up the strengths as well as the risks and limitations of any proposed match, bearing in mind that delay in placing a child who is ready to move is to be avoided if at all possible. However, it will be important to make an extra effort and take some extra time to, for example, find a family which can take a whole sibling group who are assessed as needing placement together. If efforts prove unsuccessful within the revised timescales which you have set, compromises may need to be made. These will be difficult decisions to make and should be shared by a planning group rather than resting with you and your manager alone.

Family-finding workers

Most local authorities allocate to a social worker in the adoption team the job of family finding for a particular child. There may also be a worker with marketing and publicity skills in the team who has responsibility for general recruitment of adopters and who can give advice on featuring individual children in specialist publications and other media. The agency should be looking at adopters within their consortia, from voluntary adoption agencies and through the Adoption Register as well as in-house.

Permanence planning meetings

It will be important for you to meet with these workers and to be involved in devising a plan for finding adopters for your child and in deciding who will do what. It will be important, too, to involve the child's carers in these meetings.

Your commitment to the adoption plan for your child, and your belief that there is a family out there who can meet his or her needs, are essential ingredients in a successful outcome. The family-finding social worker will really value and respond to your keenness and enthusiasm.

The child's needs

A sound knowledge of the child and of his or her needs is the basis for family finding. You and the child's foster carer should have this information and should be clear what the child's wishes and feelings are. The family finder may also want to meet the child, especially if there will need to be publicity featuring the child's need for a family. You should also discuss the case with the Adoption Support team.

The following list may be helpful to consider.

The child's wishes and feelings

What sort of direct work has been done with the child and how much remains to be done? What sense does the child make of what has happened so far and of why they can't live with their birth parents? How ready is the child to move to an adoptive family?

What sort of new family is the child envisaging? Have they expressed any clear wishes?

Identity issues

NMS 2 is about children having a positive self-view, emotional resilience and knowledge and understanding of their background. It also covers life story work. The child will also have a sense of identity in relation to their gender, their disability, if any, and their class or social background. Does the child have a clear sense of identity or are they confused about this? What has been their experience of living with people who share their background? Do their current carers share it? What work is being done to help the child to achieve a more positive sense of identity, if this is needed?

Attachment issues

What has been the child's attachment experience? How capable are they likely to be to make a good attachment to the new family? What support are the adopters likely to need?

Abuse and neglect

What has the child experienced and what has been the impact on them? Is it likely that they have experienced more abuse and neglect than is currently known about? What support are the adopters likely to need?

Behavioural issues

How does the child behave in various settings, e.g. in the foster home, at school, etc? Are there particular triggers for difficult behaviour? What strategies seem most effective for managing the behaviour? What support are the adopters likely to need?

Health and disability

What are the child's needs? Are any specialist resources required? Are there factors in the child's background which may have an impact later? Are there any practical matching considerations e.g. a child with asthma may not be able to go to a family who have pets?

Education

Does the child have additional needs? Are specialist resources required? Changes to the school admissions code mean that children adopted from care have priority for school admissions and are also eligible for the Pupil Premium. Adopters will need to inform the school that the child is adopted. In some cases, it may be better for the child to defer starting at a new school until he/she has had time to settle and attach to their new family. You will need to consider this with adopters and the school on a case-by-case basis. The most current advice on education entitlements for adopted children can be found in the Adoption Passport on the First4Adoption website.

Personality

What sort of people does the child tend to get on best with? Can anything be learned from their most successful current relationships?

Interests, hobbies, talents

What is the child really interested in or good at? Some interests may actually be more a reflection of what the foster family like doing and the child may not have had an opportunity to pursue others yet.

Physical characteristics, appearance

Are there any factors which need considering, such as a child who is or is likely to be particularly tall or short? What does the child feel about this and about the sort of family he or she would like?

The child's birth family

Do they have particular views on the sort of new family they would like for their child? While important, these should not be overriding factors.

Contact

What are the child's contact needs? Do the child and any birth relatives accept the contact plans proposed?

Support

What sorts of support are this child's adopters likely to need? A range of support services is available, from financial support to therapeutic services. An application to the Adoption Support Fund may be appropriate, and an application can be made alongside the application for the adoption order. It is worth considering what support the adopters will need in making an application. This is a rapidly changing area and current information can be found on the First4Adoption website.

Siblings

Whether siblings are to be placed together or separately should already have been decided in the planning stage based on an assessment of their needs and relationships. When a sibling group are to be placed together, their individual needs, wishes and feelings should be assessed, as described above (see section on siblings in Chapter 1, *Making a permanence plan*). There also needs to be information on the dynamics of the group and thought given to any particular skills and experiences in adoptive families which are likely to best meet the needs of the sibling group.

Other issues to consider

- Based on the child's needs, there will be some discussion of the family structures that are needed. Be as flexible as possible! It is best to welcome families in rather than exclude them. Can single or same-sex adopters meet the child's needs? Does he or she really need to be the youngest in their new family? Could there be other children in the new family? Is location important? It will be important to be as open and aware as possible about your own values and prejudices and those of others in the placement group, including the child's foster carers. It is best if these views are openly discussed at this stage rather than being left until later when potential adopters are identified. Both single and gay and lesbian carers can be a valuable resource for children but this needs to be accepted by everyone in the group.

- Some adopters wanting to adopt a sibling group have said that either the child's social worker or their own social worker has discouraged this, suggesting they take a single child first. Yet sibling groups remain amongst the hardest to place. Have you considered the panel recommendation about the adopters' strengths, and what support the adopters might need to care for a sibling group?

- The possibility of the child achieving permanence with a family member should already have been explored and discounted by this stage. However, it may be useful to have a final review. Issues around kinship care are more fully discussed in Chapter 1, *Making a permanence plan*.

- The child's wider network should also be considered. Are there adults who already have a relationship with the child and who could be considered as adopters? Crucially, do the child's current carers want to offer adoption and has this been thoroughly explored? If they would like to offer long-term fostering or special guardianship but not adoption, has this been fully considered? The role of the current carer should have been resolved by this stage but it is worth having a final review. The foster carer's involvement in the transition to a new family will be crucial. This is discussed later in this chapter.

Starting family finding

When there are no families already known to the child or in his or her network, the family-finding plan is likely to involve the following steps. It is best to search as widely as possible from the outset, but if the steps are followed in sequence it is really important that there aren't long gaps between each step.

- Considering the agency's own approved adopters and those currently being assessed.

- Considering adopters approved by agencies in the local adoption consortium.

- Referral to the Adoption Register to access approved adopters on referral from agencies in England. You can refer as soon as the ADM decision has been made, and must refer after three months if no family has been identified.

- Featuring the child in specialist family-finding services.

- Featuring the child at an Adoption Register Exchange Day or an Adoption Activity Day.

- Wider publicity in the press or on TV.

Featuring a child in family-finding publicity

Case law reported in March 2007 established the parameters for permission to "advertise" a child for adoption during care and placement order proceedings.

- A local authority must not advertise a particular child as available for adoption, or apply to a court for permission to do so, until the ADM has made the decision that adoption is the plan.

- When the adoption agency decision has been made but there is no final care order, the court is unlikely to agree to advertising, unless the plan is unopposed or there are exceptional circumstances (e.g. the mother has died or cannot be traced).

- The local authority can, at this stage, search for potential adopters of its own, via its own consortium or by referral to the Adoption Register. This does not need the court's permission.

- Where a final care order has been made and the court has expressly approved the local authority's adoption plan but a placement order has not yet been made, it is more likely that the court will look favourably on an application to advertise without needing exceptional circumstances.

- If a care order has been made, but no placement order, and the court has not yet agreed the adoption care plan (i.e. the care order was made earlier with a different care plan), the court would want to have details of the wording and location of a proposed advertisement. It would be more likely to give permission for inclusion in a specific family-finding publication or website than in more general media. In most cases the court would either grant permission for a full advertisement which identified the child and included a photo, or would refuse any advertising. It would be unlikely to sanction an anonymous advertisement.

- Once the local authority is authorised to place a child for adoption, by a placement order or the CAFCASS-witnessed consent of birth parents, no additional permission is needed for any advertising.

Responding to families

In fact, it may be that it is not necessary to feature the child widely in publicity. He or she only needs one family and if there is a family already approved by the agency or by a consortium member who seems able to meet the child's needs, you may not need to look further. If this is not the case, and the child is featured in publicity, you may get a number of families or their social workers responding.

You need to work out, with the family-finding social worker, who will respond initially to any possible families. It is *essential* that families are responded to quickly and clearly. The family finder will usually respond initially but you will need to be prepared to be involved too, and your administrator also needs to be aware of the family finding and be able to respond warmly and to take a clear message from a family.

Exchanging information on the child and family

There will usually be an initial discussion with the potential family and/or their social worker by the family finder. If the link seems as though it could be a viable one and if the family is approved, there will usually then be an exchange of reports, between workers, with the child's CPR and the adopters' report being sent. If the family isn't yet approved, the family finder will need to gather some information about them over the phone to bring to the placement planning meeting.

Considering families – the continuing role of permanence planning meetings

Whether you have one possible approved family from your own agency or a number of families who have responded to publicity about the child, it is important to arrange an early meeting for the permanence planning group to consider possible families. There may be full reports available on approved families or information on families not yet approved.

Factors to take into account in matching

It is important to keep the previously identified needs of the child as the focus when looking at what each family can offer. However, it is important, too, to keep in mind what the family's expectations seem to be and how likely it is that this child will be able to meet these. It is also important to engage the family as early as possible in the matching process. Some will already be involved, having identified a child at an Exchange or Activity Day: "chemistry" will have played a part. Adopters today are most rigorously trained and will be informed about adoption challenges from the First4Adoption website as well as their agency training. Whether the adopter or the social worker has identified the potential match, you will need to ensure that the child's needs and background are shared with them so that they can make an informed decision. You will need to consider how to explain those factors that may not be fully known, such as the risk of developmental delay or the possibility of unknown abuse.

In relation to each factor, the questions to be asked include the following:

- What are the child's needs in relation to this factor?

- How will this family meet these needs?

- What help and support will be needed and can it be offered?

In addition, consideration needs to be given to:

- What is the child able and willing to take from the new parents?

- What does this family hope to receive in return?

- What will this child be able to give back to them?

You will need to use the information already gathered on the child's needs (see earlier section in this chapter) and relate it to each family being considered.

The child's wishes and feelings

If the child still has many unresolved feelings about their birth family, is the adoptive family able to accept and work with this? What help and support will be offered in relation to any ongoing life story work?

How does this family match with the sort of new family the child is envisaging?

Identity issues

If the family does not share the child's ethnicity or cultural background, how will they meet his or her identity needs? What help and support can be offered? If the family does share the child's background but the child is confused about his or her identity and perhaps is currently placed transracially, how will the family meet the child's identity needs and what help and support could be offered? It is important to remember that the "welfare checklist" in the Adoption and Children Act requires you to consider the effect of being adopted on the child *throughout* his or her life.

Attachment issues

If the child may be very slow to make a good attachment, how prepared for this is the family? What therapeutic and other help and support can be offered?

Abuse and neglect

Is the family prepared for the impact any abuse and neglect may have had on the child? Is the family prepared for possible abuse to be disclosed later on?

Behavioural issues

What strategies seem most effective for managing the child's behaviour? Are these strategies that this family feels comfortable with? Is their approach to parenting and discipline very different from that which the child is used to, not just at home but also in his or her foster family? How will they cope with the child's possible confusion about this? Might the provision of therapeutic parenting or other support be appropriate?

Health and disability

Are any specialist resources required? If so, are they available in the family's area? Are there factors in the child's background which may have an impact later and is the family prepared for this? Have you made the prospective adopters fully aware of the child's health and developmental needs and those that might emerge later on? Are there health or disability issues in the adoptive family and what are the implications of these for the child?

Education

Are specialist resources required? If so, are they available in the family's area? Is the adopter aware of the priority access to schools, early education entitlement and the Pupil Premium (see the Adoption Passport)?

Personality

What sort of people does the child tend to get on best with? Can anything be learned from their most successful current relationships? How good is the "fit" with this family?

Interests, hobbies, talents

Does the family share any of these? Do they have interests which are very different from those of the child?

Contact

Is the adoptive family comfortable with the proposed contact arrangements? Are they prepared for the child's contact needs to change, and to manage the impact of social media on contact?

Siblings

If siblings are to be placed, are the needs of all likely to be met? Are there particular dynamics in the sibling group which need considering in relation to this family? Support, including financial, is likely to be particularly important if a large sibling group is to be placed.

Family structure

Are this child's needs compatible with those of other children in the new family? Is this family's composition likely to meet the child's needs?

Location

Are there any concerns about this?

Support

What support is planned? In relation to any gaps or deficits in the family's ability to meet the child's needs, what can be provided to help? Are there any discrepancies between what sort of support this family are asking for or are likely to need and what is proposed? Are you and the family aware of the support entitlements explained in the Adoption Passport? Adoption support is changing rapidly and you and the adopter will need to be aware of the latest developments. The Adoption Passport is updated on the First4Adoption website.

What children think is important

The Children's Rights Director asked a large number of adopted children for their views on the adoption process. This was reported on in *About Adoption: A Children's Views Report* (Morgan, 2006). One of the questions asked was what social workers should look for in choosing a family to adopt a child. These are the top ten things the children identified.

1. *That they are kind and caring*

2. *That the child is likely to get on with them and be happy*

3. *That they like children and really do want another one*

4. *That they have the same background as the child they are adopting*

5. *That they will be able to look after the child properly*

6. *That they have things in common with the child*

7. *That they understand the child's needs*

8. *That their police check is OK*

9. *That they live in the right surroundings for the child*

10. *That they will go on loving the child for ever*

Some comments were 'look for things in common', 'the personality of the child and the personality of the family must match', 'check how much time they will spend with the child'.

Visiting potential families

Consideration of the factors involved in matching can be done on paper to begin with and then a decision made about whether to visit the first choice family initially, or more than one family. If more than one family is to be visited, this needs to be made clear to them. Families can find it very hard to feel in "competition" with other families, even while recognising that finding the right family for the child must be your priority. Sensitivity is needed over this, and careful feedback given to families who are not chosen.

You will usually visit the family or families with their assessing social worker and the adoption team family-finding social worker.

It is important to remember that you are not re-assessing the family. You are considering with them:

- the child's needs and whether they can meet these;

- what their expectations are and whether the child is likely to be able to meet these;

- what sorts of help and support will be needed.

The format described in the earlier section, "Factors to take into account in matching", could form the basis for the meeting.

The family will also want to hear from you about the child and they and their worker may well have questions. It may be helpful to show them a brief film clip of the child, if you have one. They may already have met the child, or been given some information, at an Adoption Register Exchange Day or Activity Day.

There may also be additional information which you need from them or issues you want to discuss in more detail.

It is important that you are as clear as possible about when you will be meeting to decide on matching the child with a particular family so that the family know how long they will have to wait.

Moving from the consideration of several possible links to a proposed placement with one family – a match

Adoption Guidance 4.21 and 22 states that:

> *Where the agency is considering the placement of a child for adoption, it may identify a number of possible prospective adopters. It needs to compare their potential to provide a stable and permanent family for the child, based on the child's permanence report, the prospective adopter's report and other information it has collected and assessed.*

> *The agency is responsible for considering and comparing alternative prospective adopters for a particular child. In its report to the adoption panel on the proposed placement, the agency should only propose one adoptive family (that is, one couple or a single person) as the prospective adopter(s).*

The decision about which family to propose as the match for the child is a crucial one. It should not be made by you alone but should be a shared decision made at a *permanence planning meeting* and involving you and your manager, the family finder and possibly his or her manager, and with input from the child's current carers and anyone else closely involved with the child, such as a therapist.

There may well be some risks and limitations in the proposed match as well as strengths. It will be crucial to be clear about the support that can and will, realistically, be offered to address the limitations. Is this placement, with support, likely to meet the child's needs or should further family finding be undertaken? The possible harm to the child in delaying a placement and doing more family finding will need to be kept in mind.

Proposing a placement

Sharing information

Once a family has been chosen as the one whom you would like to proceed with, you must ensure that they have adequate information on which to decide whether they, too, want to proceed.

AAR 31 requires you to do the following.

- Provide the prospective adopter with a copy of the child's permanence report and any other information the agency considers relevant. Adoption Guidance 4.23–4.24 suggests that additional information could include 'reports or summaries of reports on the child's health, education or special needs. Photographs and a video film may also be helpful'. Adoption guidance further requires that the prospective adopter confirms in writing that they will keep this information confidential and will return it to the agency if requested to do so. If it is some time since the CPR was written, it is very important to provide additional up-to-date information. An adopter quoted in *Adoption – messages from inspections of adoption agencies* (CSCI, 2006) commented:

The assessment we read had very little relation to the child placed with us. This was down to the delay in our child being matched with us … they had changed so much.

- Meet with the prospective adopter to discuss the proposed placement, to get their views on it, and, specifically, to get their views on your proposed arrangements for contact with birth family or anyone else once the child is placed for adoption.

- Provide a counselling service and any further information as may be required. You will need to liaise with the family's own worker about this to ensure that the family has an opportunity to discuss and think through as fully as possible whether they are right for this child and whether the child is right for them.

- Adoption Guidance 4.8 also suggests that the adopters should be reminded of the placement planning, introduction and placement procedures. They should also be asked whether they would be willing to meet later with the child's parents, if this is considered to be appropriate.

Prospective adopters may have met the child at an Adoption Activity Day and have formed a view about him or her. The information you provide will help them better understand the child's particular issues and needs.

Involving the current foster carers

It will probably be helpful to arrange a *meeting between the prospective adopter and the child's current carers* at this stage. The carers are likely to know better than anyone what the child is like to live with and they can give valuable information to the proposed new family. However, they may need help and support to do this and it may be helpful to liaise with the carers' supervising social worker over this. Some foster carers may be tempted to minimise the child's difficulties in order to make him or her seem more "attractive" to the new family. Some may be so used to caring for looked after children that they really don't see the child as having any difficulties. Others may emphasise the child's difficulties, either because they don't want to lose him or her or because they want validation of the difficult fostering task they have undertaken. Children can behave very differently in different settings and with families who have different parenting styles and this needs to be kept in mind.

However, with these caveats, it is usually very helpful for there to be an opportunity at this stage for foster carers and prospective adopters to get to know each other, to start to form a relationship and to share information.

It will be important to have discussed the foster carer's views about different sorts of adoptive families at an earlier stage. However, if the carer still has doubts, for instance, about a single adopter for the child and a single adopter has been chosen, it may be a good idea to tell the adopter so that he or she can be prepared before meeting the carer.

Decision to proceed with the match

If, after this further period of discussion, it is decided to proceed with the match, the agency must:

- assess the adoption support needs of the child and the prospective adoptive family;

- consider the arrangements for allowing any person contact with the child;

- write an adoption placement report.

These steps are described in turn.

Assessment for adoption support needs

Undertaking an assessment of adoption support needs is a core part of adoption practice. The Adoption and Children Act 2002 is very specific about the adoption agency's responsibilities and the process that needs to be followed. That is further amplified in the Adoption Support Services Regulations 2005 and the related Statutory Guidance.

Any assessment is reliant on high quality, evidence-informed and updated information. It will build on what is already known but will reflect new or emerging issues. The assessment needs to be carried out as a partnership between the individual or the family requesting the assessment and the professionals who know them or others who have a particular expertise – health and education and other specialist areas of adoption such as contact. The assessment is aimed at exploring the issues, formulating them into description of the individual's or family's needs and, where appropriate, identifying how those needs might be met. In most circumstances, a written report must be prepared setting out these issues and the person or family must be given an opportunity to comment on that report. The procedure is set out in Regulation 14 of the ASSR 2005.

If the local authority proposes to provide adoption support services, then it must prepare a draft plan and, under Regulation 17, consult with the person or family assessed before making a final decision on the provision of that service. Following that consultation, the local authority then makes its decision about providing services and issues a notification of that decision, including the person nominated to review the plan, the outcomes from the service provided and the timescales.

The Adoption Support Fund (ASF) has become a very important source for funding for 'therapeutic interventions for the child'. The Fund has identified what is and what is not in scope, although that is under review as evidence emerges of the evidence base for such interventions. This information can be accessed through the ASF website (www.adoptionsupportfund.co.uk). It is important to note that the services that fall within the definition of adoption support go well beyond the specific definitions of the Fund and these are specified in Regulation 3 of the ASSR 2005. How any local authority meets its obligations to provide these services will be identified in its own strategic and operational objectives.

Contact arrangements

These must be detailed in the adoption placement report (Form APR). If, as they may well do, adopters require support from the agency, this must be covered in the assessment of support needs and detailed in the report.

There is more detailed information on contact, both the legislative requirements and practice issues, in Chapter 6, *Contact*.

Any restriction on exercising of parental responsibility

The prospective adopters will have parental responsibility for the child as soon as he or she is placed (unless the child is on a freeing order). However, the local authority can restrict the prospective adopters' exercise of PR and the panel is required to consider this when it considers the match. So, it is a good idea to discuss this with the adopters at this stage and to include your plans in the adoption placement report. Your adoption team and the adopters' worker will be able to help with this. There is more discussion in Chapter 13, *Supporting and supervising a placement before the adoption order*.

Adoption placement report

AAR 31 requires that an adoption placement report (Form APR) is written. This report takes the place of what used to be called a matching report. CoramBAAF has produced an electronic format for this.

The APR must include:

- the agency's reasons for proposing the placement (it may be helpful to use the "Factors to be taken into account in matching" headings described earlier in this chapter, as the basis for this part of the APR);

- the views of the prospective adopters about

    - the proposed placement

    - the arrangements the agency proposes to make for allowing any person contact with the child (but note that the child's needs may change over time);

- the proposals for the provision of adoption support services for the adoptive family;

- the arrangements the agency proposes to make for allowing any person contact with the child;

- any other relevant information. Adoption Guidance 4.29 suggests that this could, for example, include the views of the child about the proposed placement if they already know the prospective adopter.

The prospective adopter must be notified that the proposed placement is to be referred to the adoption panel. They must be given a copy of the APR and should be invited to send in any observations in writing within 10 working days (AAR 31.3).

Authorisation and agreement to place a child for adoption

Before a child can be placed for adoption the agency must have one of the following:

- a placement order made by a court;

- formal consent from the birth parent(s) witnessed by a CAFCASS officer;

- agreement by the birth parent(s) to place an infant under the age of six weeks. There is a prescribed form for this written agreement at the end of Adoption Guidance Annex B;

- a freeing order (these can no longer be applied for but an existing freeing order will remain in force unless it is revoked).

Can a child be matched with prospective adopters at panel before authorisation to place has been obtained?

Yes. AAR 32 allows a panel to consider a match at the same time as it considers the adoption plan for the child. The suitability of the prospective adopters can also be considered at the same panel. Where a child is being fostered under a Fostering for Adoption or concurrent planning placement, and the local authority is applying for a placement order, the panel will normally consider the adoption match after the placement order has been made. The Statutory Guidance *Early Permanence Placements and Approval of Prospective Adopters as Foster Parents* provides further information on the matching process, including who makes the early permanence decisions.

In other situations it is less likely to be a good idea. The child cannot be placed until the local authority is authorised to do so. There could be a delay in a court making a placement order or in getting a CAFCASS-witnessed consent. Everyone is usually geared up to plan and start introductions after a matching panel and decision but, in this case, there will have to be a wait of uncertain length, which could be quite frustrating and difficult for everyone.

Fostering for Adoption and concurrent planning placements: where a local authority intends to place a child with dually-approved carers, the nominated officer is required to make the decision to place (see the Early Permanence Statutory guidance).

The adoption panel

Full information about adoption panels and about the preparation that you need to do is given in Chapter 5, *The adoption panel*. Your manager should attend with you if possible and the family's worker will also be present, with his or her manager, if possible.

Information required

On the child

- A copy of the child's permanence report. This should include updated information as necessary to ensure it gives an accurate account of the current situation.

- Other relevant specialist reports.

- The minutes of the panel meeting that recommended the adoption plan.

On the family

- The prospective adopter's report, with any updating information as necessary.

- Minutes of the panel meeting that recommended their suitability as adopters, and any advice given by the panel on the number and age range, etc., of children for whom they could be considered.

The adoption placement report

This is described earlier in this chapter. The panel must also have the prospective adopter's observations on the report.

Attendance of prospective adopters

Regulations and guidance do not require that prospective adopters are invited to attend panel for a match. However, many local authorities do invite them and this can be very helpful. You will need to check with the agency adviser to the panel whether this can be done and, if so, what the panel process will be. It is important that the prospective adopters do not feel overwhelmed. You may want to consider how many other people will be in the room and how to put the adopters at ease.

The panel's remit

The panel is required by AAR 32 to:

- consider and recommend 'whether the child should be placed for adoption with that particular prospective adopter';

- consider and give advice to the agency about:

    – the authority's proposals for the provision of adoption support services for the adoptive family

    – the arrangements the adoption agency proposes to make for allowing any person contact with the child

    – whether the parental responsibility of any parent or guardian or the prospective adopter should be restricted and, if so, the extent of any such restriction.

This last point arises because prospective adopters are now given parental responsibility as soon as the child is placed with them (unless the child is placed on a freeing order, in which case they only get parental responsibility when an adoption order is made). However, they share this with the birth parent(s) and the local authority. The local authority must decide whether and how to restrict their exercise of it by, for example, not allowing them to agree for the child to stay away from home without them or to have invasive medical treatment. There needs to be discussion about this and some agreement reached before going to panel.

The proposed support and contact arrangements should be thought through and the availability of resources needed should be identified as it is part of the panel's job to scrutinise these arrangements carefully, and be sure that the adoptive parents have been made aware of the Adoption Passport and the Adoption Support Fund, and the right to an assessment for adoption support. Members will note any observations made by the prospective adopters. In extreme cases, if there are unresolved issues around contact or support the panel could decide to defer making a recommendation until these have been resolved. The panel should take into consideration recent changes in legislation on contact, particularly that once the child has been adopted, the adoptive parents (and certain others, including the child) can apply to the court for an order requiring or prohibiting contact. In addition, s.8 of the Children and Adoption Act 2014 amends the Children Act 1989 such that, for children in the care of the local authority, and in certain circumstances, the local authority is not required to promote contact between the child and the birth family.

Decision about the match

The decision is made following the process described in Chapter 5, *The adoption panel*. The decision-maker's decision is final. There is no statutory provision for the prospective adopter to make representations or to apply to the IRM (see Glossary) if the match is not agreed.

FURTHER READING

Betts B (2007) *A Marginalised Resource? Recruiting, assessing and supporting single carers*, London: BAAF

Byrne S (2000) *Linking and Introductions: Helping children join adoptive families*, London: BAAF

Cairns K and Cairns B (2016) *Attachment, Trauma and Resilience: Therapeutic caring for children* (2nd edn), London: CoramBAAF

Cousins J (2008) *Ten Top Tips for Finding Families for Children*, London: BAAF

Harris P (ed) (2006) *In Search of Belonging: Reflections by transracially adopted people*, London: BAAF

de Jong A and Donnelly S (2015) *Recruiting, Assessing and Supporting Lesbian and Gay Adopters*, London: BAAF

Lilley J (2016) *Our Adoption Journey: A couple's path to adoptive parenthood*, London: CoramBAAF

Morgan R (2006) *About Adoption: A children's views report*, London: CSCI

Prevatt-Goldstein B and Spencer M (2000) *"Race" and Ethnicity: A consideration of issues for black, minority ethnic and white children in family placement*, London: BAAF

Rule G (2006) *Recruiting Black and Minority Ethnic Adopters and Foster Carers*, London: BAAF

Sellick C, Thoburn J and Philpot T (2004) *What Works in Adoption and Foster Care?*, London: Barnardo's/BAAF

Selwyn J, Meakings S and Wijedasa D (2015) *Beyond the Adoption Order: Challenges, interventions and adoption disruption*, London: BAAF

Seymour N (2007) *In Black and White*, London: BAAF

Wise J (2007) *Flying Solo: A single parent's adoption story*, London: BAAF

10 Making a placement

Once the panel has recommended the match and the agency decision-maker has agreed it, there are a number of tasks which have to be undertaken. These include notifications to those affected by the decision and additions to the child's case record. An adoption placement plan must be written which details the work to be done before the placement can be made. These tasks are detailed below.

Notifications and records

AAR 33 requires that, 'as soon as possible' after this, the adoption agency must notify, in writing:

- the prospective adopter of its decision;

- the birth parents, including a father without parental responsibility if this is considered appropriate, that the child is to be placed for adoption.

It must also explain to the child what the plan is, in a way that is appropriate to the age and level of understanding of the child.

At this stage you must place on the child's case record:

- the prospective adopter's report;

- the adoption placement report and the prospective adopter's views on that report;

- the panel minutes of the case when the child was matched with the adopter;

- the record and notification of the agency's decision on the match.

For Fostering for Adoption or concurrent planning placements, Regulation 22A of the Care Planning, Placement and Case Review (England) Regulations 2010 sets out the duties with which the nominated officer must comply in making that decision.

Arrangements for placement

Adoption placement plan

This is an important document which sets out arrangements for the adoption placement. It is required by AAR 35(2). Schedule 5 to the AAR sets out what must be covered in the plan. These are:

1. *whether placed under a placement order or with the consent of the parent or guardian;*

2. *the arrangements for preparing the child and the prospective adopter for the placement;*

3. *date on which it is proposed to place the child for adoption with the prospective adopter;*

4. *the arrangements for review of the placement;*

5. *whether parental responsibility of the prospective adopter for the child is to be restricted, and if so, the extent to which it is to be restricted;*

6. *where the local authority has decided to provide adoption support services for the adoptive family, how these will be provided and by whom;*

7. *the arrangements which the adoption agency has made for allowing any person contact with the child, the form of contact, the arrangements for supporting contact and the name and contact details of the person responsible for facilitating the contact arrangements (if applicable);*

8. *the dates on which the child's life story book and later life letter are to be passed by the adoption agency to the prospective adopter (Adoption NMS 2.8 states that the prospective adopters receive the letter within ten working days of the adoption ceremony);*

9. *details of any other arrangements that need to be made;*

10. *contact details of the child's social worker, the prospective adopter's social worker and out of hours contacts (AAR 35 (2)).*

CoramBAAF has produced Form APP for writing an adoption placement plan which can be accessed from your adoption team or from www.corambaaf.org.uk in the members' area.

It is suggested in Adoption Guidance 5.3 that the agency should prepare a draft of this plan, which can form the basis for the placement planning meeting with the prospective adopter. As you can see from the list of required items, most of them will already have been discussed and included in the adoption placement report, which was presented to the panel. The panel will have considered, and may have given advice on, any proposed restriction in the adopter's exercise of parental responsibility, the proposed support arrangements and the proposed contact arrangements, and you should consider, and may want to include, these points in the draft adoption placement plan.

There is fuller discussion in subsequent sections of this chapter on the preparation of the child and of the prospective adopter for the placement, on planning introductions, on contact and support arrangements and on the adopter's parental responsibility. There is also a section on the life story book and later life letter.

Placement planning meeting

This should take place as soon as possible after the matching decision. This is likely to be some days after the panel, which will give the prospective adopters time to start getting used to the idea that the child really is going to be placed with them. If the placement is an inter-agency one and the prospective adopters and their worker have travelled some distance to get to the panel, it may be necessary to have the planning meeting on that day or the next one. However, this should be avoided if possible and left until after the decision has been made.

Adoption Guidance 5.4 suggests the people who should attend the meeting, in addition to yourself, are:

*   the prospective adopter(s);
*   their social worker;
*   the child's current carer;
*   any relevant specialists;
*   the foster carer's supervising social worker, if appropriate.

It may well be appropriate also to invite the family-finding social worker, adoption manager and your manager. Either the adoption manager or your manager would usually chair the meeting.

A provisional draft of the adoption placement plan will form the basis of the meeting. Each item should be gone through, discussed, agreed and recorded.

CoramBAAF has forms designed to be used in inter-agency placements, to summarise information which needs to be shared, to record who will do what and to record plans for introductions. Form IA details financial arrangements between the family's and the child's agency and is designed to be used by the two sets of agency workers. Form APR will involve the prospective adopters and the current carers too. The adoption workers in your agency should be familiar with these forms and may use them for in-house placements too.

National Minimum Standards for Adoption, Standard 12.9, requires that:

The adoption agency ensures that the adopters understand the importance for the birth family to be told if their child dies during childhood or soon afterwards and agrees to notify the adoption agency. The prospective adopters' decision and any subsequent action are recorded on their case record.

It may well also be appropriate to ask adopters to agree in writing as to whether they would want to be told:

- if a birth parent or close birth family member dies;

- if significant health issues come to light in the birth family;

- if another child is born to the birth parents.

This isn't a required part of the adoption placement plan but it may be appropriate to include a discussion of these points at the placement planning meeting and to record the results in the adoption placement plan.

After the placement planning meeting

As soon as possible after the placement planning meeting, the adoption placement plan should be completed, as agreed at the meeting, and a final version sent to the prospective adopter(s).

The prospective adopter(s) must then formally notify the adoption agency that they want to proceed with the placement.

Authorisation or agreement to place a child for adoption

Before a child can be placed for adoption the agency must have one of the following:

- a placement order made by a court;

- formal consent from the birth parent(s) or guardians and from anyone who is a special guardian by virtue of a special guardianship order made by a court, witnessed by a CAFCASS officer;

- agreement by the birth parent(s) to place an infant under the age of six weeks (there is a prescribed form for this written agreement at the end of Adoption Guidance Annex B);

- a freeing order (these can no longer be applied for but an existing freeing order will remain in force unless it is revoked by a court).

Preparation and support

Preparing and supporting the child

A required section in the adoption placement plan is 'The arrangement for preparing the child … for the placement'. Some thought will thus have been given to this when the draft plan was prepared and when the final plan was agreed with the prospective adopters at the placement planning meeting.

This work should flow on from the life story work which should already be being done. The child may be well aware that prospective adopters have been identified but a younger child may not be.

It will almost certainly be you, with the support of the child's foster carers, who tells the child about the specific prospective adopters. They will probably have prepared a little book about themselves for the child, with photos and brief details, which can be shared and gone through. Some prospective adopters also prepare a short film clip.

It is really important not to rush this stage. The child will probably need some time to get used to the information and to ask questions.

The Children's Rights Director gathered the views of adopted children and published the results in *About Adoption: A Children's Views Report*. The survey reported the top ten things children want to be told about their adoptive families.

1. *What sort of people they are*

2. *The number of children and young people in the family*

3. *Where they live*

4. *Their personality and beliefs*

5. *Reassurance that they want you and are friendly towards children*

6. *Their family background*

7. *Why they want to adopt you*

8. *If they have any pets*

9. *If they have a story book or DVD about the family*

10. *If they will have contact with my birth family.* (Morgan, 2006)

Some children would like to have been told more than they were about:

- what their adoptive parents' life was like;

- the personalities of their adoptive parents;

- what other relations the adoptive parents had whom you would be meeting.

Preparing and supporting the adopters

It is also required that the adoption placement plan includes information on 'The arrangements for preparing … the prospective adopter for the placement'.

Again, this will have been thought about and discussed during the formulation of the plan. The prospective adopters will already have a copy of the child's CPR and other extensive information. You could liaise with their worker about whether other information is needed.

This is also the stage where the prospective adopters and the child's foster carers can get to know each other better, having probably already met, and the foster carers can share as much information as possible about the child.

The adopters will need to make practical arrangements about leaving or taking time off work, about school or other provisions the child needs, and about preparing the child's room. It is also important that they have time to prepare their wider family, including, crucially, any other children whom they have. Their own worker should be available to offer them help and support.

Child appreciation day

An increasing number of local authorities are finding a child appreciation day to be a good investment of time at this stage. This is an opportunity to invite people who have known the child – such as former foster carers, teachers, nursery staff, health visitors, former social workers, birth family members if appropriate – to meet with prospective adopters and current carers and professionals, to share their experiences of caring for and working with the child. This can give a very vivid, "living" picture of the child at different periods and with different people. It can help identify patterns in the child's history and possible developmental issues that may arise.

Prospective adopters report that they find this day invaluable in gaining information about the child and making links. Notes of people's contributions and any photos or memorabilia which they have brought will be a valuable addition to the life story material which the child and the adopters already have.

Your adoption team or CoramBAAF can give information on setting up a child appreciation day (see also Sayers and Roach, 2011).

Supporting the foster carers

It is stressful and distressing for most foster carers when a child whom they have cared for, perhaps for many months or longer, moves to prospective adopters. This is likely to be the case however much they want the child to move on to adopters and however much they like the adopters. However, sometimes carers are much more ambivalent, having wanted to keep the child long term or having some doubts about the prospective adopters.

It is important to give time for foster carers and prospective adopters to get to know each other, as described in Chapter 9.

The foster carers and their family are likely to need support in the vital but demanding task of helping the child to move on. They will value and appreciate your acknowledgement of their feelings and your involvement of them in planning and managing the move. However, their supervising social worker should be their main support and you will need to liaise with him or her, to ensure that they do offer this extra support. Thought should be given to what the expectations are of continued contact for the child with their foster carer, as this has been highlighted in research as important to children.

Adoption support services

There was an assessment of these at the matching stage and information on proposed services will have been included in the APR. Arrangements now need to be agreed, although there will still be an opportunity to review them after placement.

The provision of *financial* support is governed by the Adoption Support Regulations. Adoption Statutory Guidance covers the assessment of financial support and what the local authority may or may not means test.

Detailed information on adoption support is given in Chapter 7, *Adoption support services*.

Contact

Contact arrangements will have been discussed and hopefully agreed at the matching stage. However, the panel may have given helpful advice and plans may be amended at this adoption placement plan stage.

Work with the birth family

You will have an important role in supporting the birth family in relation to the adoption and in relation to contact arrangements. A meeting between the adopters and the birth parent(s) or other significant family members can be very helpful. It needs to be carefully arranged though and both sets of parents will need a support worker present. It will be a good idea to discuss and plan the questions and answers beforehand, to some extent, so that neither the birth parents nor the adopters are tempted by the emotion of the meeting to say more than they want to. You will need to talk to the birth parents about what they want to ask and to say and then liaise with the adopters' worker about this. It can offer an invaluable opportunity for the parents to come alive for each other and can offer reassurance for both.

The child's birth parents or other relatives may also want to write a letter for the child about themselves and their family, about their relationship with the child and about why the child is being adopted. You can offer help and support so that this letter is as helpful for the child as possible.

Introductions – plan and review

It is required that the adoption placement plan includes the 'date on which it is proposed to place the child for adoption with the prospective adopter'.

The work to be done before the child can be placed should be discussed and agreed at a placement planning meeting before the adoption placement plan is finalised. As already discussed, there is important preparation work to be done with the child and with the prospective adopters. This should not be rushed, and it may be that the "proposed" placement date will need to be reviewed in the light of this work.

The purpose of introductions is to enable a child and prospective adopters to start to get to know each other and to "practise" being together. There needs to be a gradual transfer of trust and love and of parenting tasks from the foster carers to the adopters. In general, young children probably manage best with a short, intensive period of introductions over a week or ten days, while children over about three will probably need longer, including an opportunity to spend time in the adopter's home. However, it is important *not* to have rigid ideas on what is right. Each introductions plan must be agreed by adopters and foster carers but must be designed to meet the needs of the individual child.

It is best to avoid placements before festive seasons or other times when the family's normal routines may be disrupted and when social work and other support may be less available. Introductions should also not be arranged around adult deadlines, like foster carers going on holiday, if at all possible.

CoramBAAF's Form APP is designed to help in formulating and recording an introductions plan.

It is important to build in an opportunity to review how the relationship-building is going before a decision is made to place the child. It is important that you, and others, share any doubts and concerns that you may have. In the Part 8 Review of a placement which went disastrously wrong when a child of four was killed while in the care of his prospective adopters, there were already some concerns raised about and by the prospective adopters in the introductory period. In retrospect, the Review recommended that it would have been a good idea to call "time out", and reduce the pace of introductions, delaying the move. This would have given the workers concerned an opportunity to do further assessment and preparation work.

Children commented, in the Children's Views Report already mentioned, that the best ways of getting to know your adoptive family are:

1. *Visiting and staying a few days before moving in*

2. *Going on days out with the family*

3. *Spending time talking with your future adoptive parents*

4. *Being given a video or book about the family*

5. *Having fun and playing games with the family* (Morgan, 2006)

The life story book and later life letter

The dates on which the child's life story book and later life letter are to be given by the adoption agency to the prospective adopter must be set down in the adoption placement plan.

It is to be hoped that these could be given to the adopter at placement. However, if this is not possible, a date should be set as soon as possible. The *life story book* is particularly crucial. It can form a reassuring link for the child between his or her life up to now and their new life with their adoptive family. The child may want to refer to it and needs to be confident that their prospective adopters are aware of, and accepting of, the information it contains. They can add to it, about the child's life with them, emphasising that there is some continuity for the child. There is more information on life story books in Chapter 2, *Working with the child*.

The *later life letter* could be sent on later. Adoption NMS 2.8 states that the prospective adopters receive the letter within ten working days of the adoption ceremony. It should not contain any significant information that the prospective adopters do not already have, either in the CPR or other reports, or in the life story book. Adoption Guidance 5.48 states that 'The child's life story book helps them explore and understand their early history and life before adoption'. It should give the child information about the birth family and help the child understand why he or she couldn't live with them and was adopted.

The letter is a direct communication from you, the social worker, to the child for when the child is older. However, it should be open to the adopters and should not in any way be information that goes behind their backs to the child. In general, they should decide what it would be helpful for the child to know and when, using all the information they have, and getting support from the local authority when necessary. They will decide when to give the letter to the child, unless he or she is already old enough to be given it by you.

You may know the child very well and have shared experiences of your work together which you could write down. You may also have information about your contact with their birth family which you could put in the letter. At its best, the letter is a communication from you to the child about your work together or about your contact with the child if he or she is very young. It will also contain information and perhaps anecdotes about their birth parents and about your work with them. It may be more detailed than a life story book and it will be more personal than a CPR or other reports. However, in some cases, if you don't know the child or the birth parents well, it may be best to keep the letter fairly brief and to refer the child/young person back to their life story book and to the more detailed information which their adoptive parents will have. For more information on writing a later life letter, see Moffat, 2012.

Other requirements

Notifications prior to placement

AAR 35(6) requires the agency to:

- Send to the prospective adopter's GP written notification of the proposed placement and a written report on the child's health history and current state of health.

  You will need to liaise with the medical adviser as he or she will normally do this.

- Send to the local authority (if this is not your agency) written notification of the proposed placement.

  This will be particularly important if this local authority is not the family's approving authority either. It will be helpful if your adoption team or adoption support worker liaises with the adoption team in this local authority about support services. Check with the adoption team as they may well send this notification.

- Send to the Primary Care Trust, in whose area the prospective adopter has their home, written notification of the proposed placement.

  Again, liaise with the medical adviser and adoption team as one of them will usually send this notification.

- Where the child is of compulsory school age, send to the local education authority in whose area the prospective adopter has their home, written notification of the proposed placement and information about the child's educational history and whether he or she has been or is likely to be assessed for special education needs.

- There is no formal requirement to notify the child's birth parents of the date of the placement for adoption. Whether or not you decide to do this will depend on the individual situation.

A child who is already living with the prospective adopter

When a child has been living with a foster carer who has now been matched with him or her for adoption, AAR 35.5 requires that a date must be set for the formal placement for adoption and the prospective adopter informed of this in writing. This is likely to be a significant date for both the child and the prospective adopter and their family even though, in practical terms, nothing much changes. They may want to mark or celebrate it in some way.

Changes to the adoption placement plan

Any changes to the placement plan must be notified in writing to the prospective adopter (AAR 35 (7)). They should, of course, also be discussed and agreed with the adopter.

Records

AAR 35.8 requires that you add the following to the child's case record.

- a copy of the placement agreement if the child is less than six weeks old; and
- a copy of the adoption placement plan and any changes to the plan.

FURTHER READING

Argent H (2011) *Related by Adoption: A handbook for grandparents and other relatives* (2nd edn), London: BAAF

Argent H (2006) *Ten Top Tips for Placing Children in Permanent Families*, London: BAAF

Byrne S (2000) *Linking and Introductions: Helping children join adoptive families*, London: BAAF

Carr K (2007) *Adoption Undone*, London: BAAF

Fahlberg V (1994) *A Child's Journey Through Placement*, London: BAAF

Lilley J (2016) *Our Adoption Journey: A couple's path to adoptive parenthood*, London: CoramBAAF

Moffat F (2012) *Writing a Later Life Letter*, London: BAAF

Morgan R (2006) *About Adoption: A children's views report*, London: Commission for Social Care Inspection

Sayers A and Roach R (2011) *Child Appreciation Days*, London: BAAF

BOOKS FOR USE WITH CHILDREN

Foxon J (2001) *Nutmeg Gets Adopted*, London: BAAF

Lidster A (2012) *Chester and Daisy Move On*, London: BAAF

11 Placing a child with prospective adopters who live overseas

For many years, a small number of looked after children have been placed for adoption with relatives living overseas. With the increasing mobility of families and increased recognition of the importance of trying to keep children within their extended family, these placements are becoming more common. The arrangements will vary according to whether the country where the relatives live has ratified the Hague Convention. The Adoptions with a Foreign Element Regulations 2005 (FER) set out the requirements for Hague Convention adoptions. However, adoption guidance states that similar practice should be followed for adoptions involving other non-Hague Convention countries. These situations are complex and you should definitely take advice from your legal department and contact the Central Authority for England as early as possible. Getting the process wrong may mean that the child cannot enter the country. An adoption order is the only order which most countries recognise. A special guardianship order may be recognised in some countries but not in others.

The Hague Convention

This is the shorthand description of the Convention on Protection of Children and Co-operation in respect of Intercountry Adoption. It was concluded in the Hague (Netherlands) in May 1993 and was finally ratified by the UK on 1 June 2003. Many other countries have ratified and implemented the Convention and new ones are doing so regularly. It is possible to check on whether the Convention is in force in a particular country on www.hcch.net.

The day-to-day administration of the Central Authority in England is discharged by the intercountry adoption team at the DfE. You should contact them as soon as you think that you may want to place a child with relatives overseas, as there are detailed procedures to follow. In addition, the Intercountry Adoption Centre (a voluntary adoption agency) can provide general advice.

Considering the extended family

This should be a routine stage when looking for a permanent new family for a child. There needs to be discussion with the child's birth parents and others about who might be able to offer a home to the child. If relatives living overseas are suggested, you need to explore, as much as you can, whether this might be a viable option. Contact by phone, email, letter or Skype (or similar) will be important.

Working with foreign authorities where a child has links to a foreign country

(This text is reproduced from pp198–199 in *Making Good Assessments* (Beesley, 2015))

In cases where a child has links to a foreign country, a number of issues need to be considered before the agency commences (or arranges for) an assessment of possible family/friends carers living overseas, or before it decides to place the child with non-related carers in the UK, or determines whether it needs to notify the relevant foreign authorities.

In 2014, the Department for Education (DfE) published the advice, *Working with Foreign Authorities: Child protection cases and care orders*. The advice is likely to be needed by social workers when they are:

- carrying out an assessment under s.47 of the Children Act 1989, where the child has links to a foreign country, in order to understand the child's case history and/or to engage with the family;

- when a child with links to a foreign country becomes the subject of a child protection plan, has required immediate protection, or is made subject to care proceedings, the social worker should consider informing the relevant foreign authority; and

- contacting or assessing potential carers abroad (such as extended family members).

It also states that:

It is inadvisable for a social worker from England to travel overseas to work on cases unless they have first contacted the relevant foreign authority. The qualifications of social workers from England may not be automatically recognised overseas, and it is therefore important to check that the social worker has the appropriate licences and legal cover to undertake the work.

There may therefore be occasions when an agency needs to work with or through another agency.

There are two related advice notes: *Advice on Placement of Looked After Children across Member States of the European Union* (DfE, 2013), and *Cross-Border Child Protection Cases: The 1996 Hague Convention* (DfE, 2012)

Agencies may also wish to refer to guidance issued by the President of the Family Division: President's Guidance of 10 November 2014: *The International Child Abduction and Contact Unit* (ICACU).

It is important to involve the overseas authorities as early as possible, as they may have the right to ask for proceedings to be brought in their own country. If they become involved partway through proceedings, this will result in a jurisdictional argument followed by possible transfer and creating significant delay for the child.

Placing a child for adoption by relatives overseas

Where the local authority is considering placing the child for adoption by relatives overseas, the adoption should proceed under the terms of the Hague Convention of 29 May 1993 on Protection of Children and Co-operation in Respect of Intercountry Adoption, where the relatives live in a country that has also implemented that Convention. If the relatives' country has not implemented the Convention, a similar process is followed. Agencies in England and Wales will need to comply with the Adoptions with a Foreign Element Regulations 2005, and relevant statutory guidance. The agency should contact the Central Authority (CA) for adoption (there is a CA in each of England, Wales, Scotland, Northern Ireland and the Isle of Man) at the earliest opportunity. The CA will be able to advise further on the procedures.

Counselling and informing the child

In addition to the counselling and preparation work described in Chapter 2, *Working with the child*, you are required, by FER 36, to counsel the child about the plan to place him or her in a family overseas. You should explain this as clearly as you can and confirm this in writing. This is a required process if the country overseas is a Convention one and Adoption Guidance requires this for other countries too.

Counselling and informing the birth parents

The counselling requirements about the adoption plan are as described in Chapter 3, *Working with the birth family*. In addition, you are required, by FER 37, to counsel and inform the child's parents about the plan to place him or her in a family overseas. This needs to be confirmed in writing.

Role of the panel in approving the plan

The child and the birth parents must have been informed and counselled about the plan.

The child's CPR must include:

- a summary of the possibilities for placement within the UK (FER 38(a));

- an assessment of whether an adoption by a person in a particular country is in the child's best interests.

Where there is parental consent to adoption, you may ask the panel to recommend the plan to place the child overseas before you have a full report on the prospective adopters or you may take a plan, a possible approval and a match to the same panel.

Role of the panel in approval of family and matching

The report on the assessment of the family, which may have been prepared by social workers in the relatives' country, will need to be presented to the panel for a recommendation about approval, before the family can be matched with the child. If the report has not been prepared by your social workers, you should make the panel aware of this, and of any particular issues you consider that the panel should take into consideration.

If an Article 15 report has been prepared in a Hague Convention country, it is only a match which will need to be considered by your panel.

Support arrangements

The Adoption Support Services Regulations 2005 will not apply overseas, although financial support can still be given. It will be important to liaise with welfare/adoption agencies in the country from early on in the process to see what support may be available and whether there will be any charge for this.

Contact arrangements

How will these be facilitated? Will support be needed to arrange or finance contact? It will be important to liaise with a local agency in the adopter's country if any support or supervision may be required for contact which takes place in that country.

Making the placement

Before a Hague Convention adoption placement can proceed, the local authority must inform the Central Authority for England at the Department for Education (DfE), which will formally notify its counterpart in the adopter's country. A decision is then made to proceed.

In all cases, the child must live with the prospective adopters for at least 10 weeks before either a Convention adoption order can be made in England or for parental responsibility to be granted under s.84 of the Adoption and Children Act 2002 prior to making the Convention order overseas. In *Re A (A Child) [2009] EWCA Civ 41*, the Court of Appeal held that the 10 week period could be partly or fully fulfilled by the time spent with the prospective adopters in their home abroad.

If two people are applying to adopt, both must live with the child in this 10 week period. They can then apply to the High Court for parental responsibility. They are not able to take the child out of the country unless this has been granted (Adoption and Children Act 2002, ss.84 and 85).

If the 10 week period is to be in the UK, arrangements will need to be made for accommodation to be provided for them. Regular visits and reviews should take place during this period.

Leaving the UK

Once parental responsibility under Section 84 is granted to the adopters, they are able to leave the UK and return with the child to their own country. The Section 84 order extinguishes the parental responsibility of everyone else, i.e. the birth parent(s) and the local authority. The child is no longer a looked after child. Although the Section 84 order is the same, in many ways, as an adoption order, most prospective adopters will apply for a full adoption order on their return home as this is the only order recognised by virtually all countries.

There is no requirement under the Hague Convention for post-placement reports to be provided. You should consider what, if any, reports you may want to receive, at what frequency, for how long, and discuss this with the prospective adopters and the overseas Central Agency.

Placing a child overseas with "stranger" adopters

It is possible to place a looked after child with 'stranger' adopters who have been assessed and approved in a Hague Convention country, although this is very rare. This would mirror the adoption by UK residents of a child from overseas.

The process would be largely the same as that for placing a child with relatives overseas.

- The child and his or her parents would need to be informed and counselled about the plan to try to find adopters overseas.

- A report would need to be prepared for the panel including the efforts made to find adopters in the UK and the reasons why a placement overseas in a particular country is in the child's best interests.

- Once an agency decision is made, the child's details would be forwarded to the Department for Education (DfE) which provides the Central Authority (CA) services for England. The CA would then arrange for brief anonymised details of the child to be placed on its Convention list of children in England available for intercountry adoption.

- Families overseas who are assessed and approved to adopt from the UK will have their papers forwarded by their country's Central Authority to the CA.

- The CA will do a fairly basic check with any waiting child, based on age, gender and whether the child is part of a sibling group.

- The CA will send the family's papers to the local authority for a possible child.

- The child's agency will consider the match, requesting any additional information via the CA.

- If the match seems possible, it will be considered by the adoption panel and a decision subsequently made.

- A report on the child will then be prepared and sent, via the CA and the overseas Central Authority, to the prospective adopters.

- If they decide to proceed, they will travel to the UK to meet the social workers and the child.

- If everyone is happy to proceed, the local authority must inform the CA which will liaise with the other Central Authority. A decision will then be made to proceed and the required consents exchanged.

- The prospective adopters must live with the child for 10 weeks before they can apply to the High Court for parental responsibility and leave to take the child overseas or for an adoption order to be made under the terms of the Hague Convention in the UK.

- No children in England have so far been identified for adoption overseas to "stranger" adopters. It is difficult to envisage the sort of child for whom this might be appropriate. It is most likely to be considered in cases where it will enable a child to be placed with adopters overseas who match the child's ethnicity and heritage. For instance, for a child born to people visiting or living in the UK but retaining strong links to their country of origin, it might be appropriate to consider adoption for the child with adopters in that country.

12 Placing a relinquished infant for adoption

In some agencies, work with a pregnant woman who is considering adoption for her baby is done in the adoption team. However, in others it is done by child care teams. If the latter is the case in your agency, it will be important to liaise with the adoption team, to get any help or advice which they can offer. CoramBAAF has an advice note, *Pregnant and Thinking about Adoption?*, which is likely to be helpful for the woman concerned. There is useful guidance to this work in Chapter 2 of the Adoption Guidance and the other chapters in this book are relevant too. The same regulations apply and must be followed, albeit in a somewhat concertinaed form.

Pre-birth counselling

Pre-birth counselling should be offered to the woman from as early as possible and she should be encouraged to think through her choices, which are:

- to keep the baby, with whatever support may be available from her wider family and from your agency and other organisations;

- to place the baby for adoption;

- to consider terminating the pregnancy.

You will need to explain the legal implications of adoption and the procedure for placing the child and for gaining consent (see later in this section).

You will probably be very used to working with birth parents where there are child protection concerns about their care of their children. You will be involved in making difficult decisions about removing a child from the care of parents who want to continue parenting them. Work with relinquishing birth mothers (and fathers) is very different. The parents may be well able to offer good care to their baby. However, they are making the decision that they would like the child to be adopted. Many birth mothers who consider this do, in fact, change their mind and decide to keep their baby, often soon after the birth. If this is the case, you will need to offer whatever support you can. Other parents will remain clear that they do want their child adopted and it is important that arrangements are made for this as soon as possible.

Involving the birth father

You should try to see and counsel the birth father, if at all possible, even if he does not have parental responsibility. It is important to know what his views about the adoption plan are and also to gather information about him which the child may find useful later on.

His formal consent to adoption will need to be sought if he has parental responsibility for the child. He will have this:

- If he is married to the mother, or was married to her when the baby was conceived;

- If he is named on the birth certificate;

- If he makes a parental responsibility agreement with the mother or gets a parental responsibility order from a court after the birth.

If he does not have parental responsibility, his formal consent to adoption is not needed but his views should still be sought if possible.

If he is married to the mother but is not the father of the child, the court may accept formal evidence that he is not the father and that therefore his consent to adoption is not needed.

If the birth mother does not want the father involved, you will need to consult with your legal department. Case law *Re L* and *Re C*, in *Adoption & Fostering*, Volume 31:4 (2007), has clarified that a woman cannot be forced to reveal the father's name, although she should be encouraged to do so. If the father is known, but she does not want him contacted, your legal department will advise whether Directions may need to be sought from court about this. Whether or not he is contacted will depend partly on the nature of the relationship and on whether there might be any safety issues involved for the mother or child.

If a birth father is contacted and wants to care for the child himself or with his family, this could be arranged. However, if the birth mother is against this, the birth father will need to apply to court, probably for a child arrangements order, and the court will need to decide on the best option for the child.

Involvement of extended family

There is no absolute requirement for extended family to be contacted. However, this should be done if at all possible. This would be to explore the possibility of the baby being cared for by a relative, to explore the support the family might give to parents to enable them to care for the child, and to gather information on the family which might be helpful to the child later on.

In case law, reported in *Adoption & Fostering*, 31:2 (2007), the Court of Appeal held that the birth father's parents should be contacted, even though the father was against this. The court held that the child had a right to be brought up within her family unless there was good reason why not. It seemed probable in this case that the grandparents might consider caring for the child. To deprive a significant member of the family of knowledge of the child's existence was a fundamental step which could only be justified on compelling grounds.

However, this contrasted with an earlier case reported in Volume 30:4 (2006) when birth parents succeeded in their request for extended family members not to be told of the birth of their baby. In that case the court was satisfied of the likely negative reaction of both sets of grandparents and the probability that they would not wish to care for the child themselves.

Two further cases are reported on in *Adoption & Fostering*, Volume 31:4 (2007), *re L* and *re C*. In both cases the Court of Appeal came to the conclusion that neither the birth father nor the extended family need be contacted, given that both birth mothers were adamant that they did not want them contacted.

However, this remains a complex and difficult area. If birth parents do not want you to contact their extended family, you will need to find out why and encourage them to agree. You will also need to contact your legal department as an approach to the court for Directions on this may be necessary.

Arrangements for placement

Adoption Guidance 2.50 and 2.51 suggest that, when parents have been counselled pre-birth and adoption is considered the preferred option, work should start on the child's permanence report and arrangements should be made for 'the agency medical adviser and adoption panel to be ready to consider the case as soon as possible after the child is born; and begin family finding so that the baby can be placed for adoption with prospective adopters once the decision-maker has decided that the child should be placed for adoption and placed with those specific prospective adopters'. Section 2.52 adds that, 'With enough preparation the adoption panel should be ready to consider the case within a day or so of the birth'.

The birth mother, and birth father if he is involved, would need to be counselled after the birth to check whether they still want adoption. If they do, the CPR and health report can be completed for presentation to panel. Panel considers all cases where there is parental consent, unless the local authority is also seeking a care order.

Prospective adopters can be considered before the child is born. However, a formal matching at panel can only happen once the child is born.

Choosing and involving adopters

Your adoption team will need to be alerted and involved as soon as possible, certainly before the birth if adoption seems a likely outcome. You will need to talk to the birth parent(s) about the sort of adopters whom they would like for their child and you will need to draw up some matching factors, as discussed in Chapter 9, *Finding a family and making a match*. The adoption team will need to ensure that any prospective adopters who may be linked with an infant under six weeks old understand the added risks in terms of no formal consent at that stage and limited health and developmental information.

Meeting between birth parent(s) and adopters

It can be extremely useful to have a meeting between birth parent(s) and prospective adopters. This will be highly emotional and needs careful planning. You should be there to support the birth parent(s) and the prospective adopters' worker should be present too. The meeting should normally be after the formal matching decision has been made after panel but should be before the child is placed, if possible. It will enable an exchange of information and for both sets of parents to become "real" for each other. A photo of them together could be helpful for the child later on.

Timing of the placement

When babies routinely stayed in hospital for up to ten days after birth, it was possible to place them directly from hospital to adopters. Now that babies are usually discharged very soon after birth, this is unlikely to be possible, although just might be, as described above.

It will probably be more likely that the infant will need to be accommodated and placed in foster care for a short period before moving on to adopters. However, it really is important that this is only for a *short* period, a matter of weeks only, if possible. If the baby's parent(s) have been counselled and are still clear after the birth that they want the baby to be adopted, there should be no delay. The baby needs to be settled with his or her adoptive parents as soon as possible.

Some parents may be unsure what they want once the baby is born. You will need to offer them the opportunity to talk and think this through, perhaps involving someone from your adoption team. However, you must be mindful that the baby needs to be settled with their permanent parent, whether this is their birth mother or an adoptive parent, as soon as possible. The baby should not linger in temporary foster care any longer than necessary and the parents need to be aware of this. If, as sometimes happens, the mother becomes impossible to contact, you will need to consult with the IRO and with the legal department about the possibility of applying for a placement order to enable you to place the child for adoption.

Consent to placement for adoption of a child under six weeks old

Birth mothers are not able to consent formally to placement for adoption until the baby is at least six weeks old. However, it is possible for the agency to place a baby younger than this for adoption.

There is an agreement form for this which should be used. It is in Annex B to the Adoption Guidance and your adoption team should be able to give you a copy or it can be accessed from www.corambaaf.org.uk or from www.everychildmatters.gov.uk/adoption.

Formal consent under s.19 of the Act will need to be obtained as soon as the baby is six weeks old (see Chapter 8, *Authorisation to place a child for adoption – placement orders and conesent* for more information).

The birth mother's agreement to placement before six weeks and formal consent after this, and that of the birth father if he has parental responsibility, must be sought whatever their age. This is the legally valid consent even if they are under sixteen.

Can a birth parent make their own adoption placement?

It is legal for a mother or for a father with parental responsibility, if both parents agree, to place a child for adoption with the child's brother, sister, uncle, aunt or grandparent. The relative will need to apply to a court for an adoption order. The child must have lived with them for three years before they can do this, although they can, and presumably would, apply to the court for leave to apply sooner. A report from the local authority where the relative lives will be needed at that point.

The parent(s) and the relatives might want to discuss a possible placement with you and this could be helpful. However, you are not able to prevent the placement unless there are grounds for care proceedings. You might want to discuss other legal options such as special guardianship as a possible alternative to adoption.

It is unlawful for parents to make their own private adoption placement with people other than the close relatives listed above. If parents have a particular wish for their child to be placed with a more distant relative or a friend, it may sometimes be possible for that person to be assessed and approved as a prospective adopter. However, this will take time. You will need to liaise with your adoption team immediately if a relinquishing birth parent makes this request.

Legal consequences of the placement for adoption by an adoption agency of a child under six weeks, in the period before formal consent is given

- If the parents or guardians change their minds, the child must be returned by the agency within seven days, unless the local authority applies for a placement order. This application exempts the local authority from the duty to return the child until the application is determined by the court. However, the same grounds as for a care order would have to exist.

- Contact is at the discretion of the local authority, or a s.26 contact order can be made by a court.

- Neither the local authority nor the prospective adopters have parental responsibility.

FURTHER READING

BAAF (2006) *Pregnant and Thinking about Adoption?*, London: BAAF

Cousins J and Morrison M with de Sousa S (2003) *Right from the Start: Best practice in adoption planning for babies and other children*, London: BAAF

13 Supporting and supervising a placement before the adoption order

Visits after placement

Regulatory requirements

When a child is placed with prospective adopters, the agency must ensure:

> ... that the child and the prospective adopters are visited within one week of the placement and thereafter at least once a week until the first review and thereafter at such frequency as the agency decides at each review. (AAR 36)

A written report must be made of the visits and the prospective adopter must be provided with 'such advice and assistance' as the agency considers necessary.

Who should visit

Who should visit and when should be discussed and agreed with the adopters at the placement planning meeting. You will need to discuss this with the family's worker. Adoption Guidance 5.25 states that:

> visits should be shared wherever possible between the child's social worker and prospective adopter's social worker and it is essential that there is clarity from the outset about which social worker will conduct each visit and that they communicate promptly with each other, including sharing their written reports.

Prospective adopters are likely to value contact with the adoption team worker who has assessed them and whom they know. However, the child is likely to want to see the social worker whom they know. It will be likely to be helpful for the prospective adopters too to have contact with the worker who knows the child and is familiar with their history and with how they were in their previous foster home.

Seeing the child

Adoption Guidance 5.26 states that:

> The child's social worker has the primary responsibility for ensuring the child's welfare and should on each visit see and speak to the child alone. The exceptions to this are:
>
> • where the child refuses (and is of sufficient age and understanding to refuse);
>
> • where the social worker considers it inappropriate to do so (again having regard to the child's age and understanding); and

- *where the social worker is unable to do so, for example because the child is out.*

This responsibility can be shared with the adopters' social worker, who would need to record their visit for the child's file.

This will need to be handled sensitively. Prospective adopters at this stage may well be feeling quite unsure and anxious about how to fulfil their new parenting responsibilities. They need help and support in bonding with the child and in becoming adoptive parents. However, the child may have concerns or anxieties which he or she would be unsure about sharing in the presence of the adopters, and the opportunity to do this with a social worker who, it is to be hoped, he or she already knows well and trusts, should be given.

What should be covered in visits

AAR 36 sets out what should be covered in the review once a child is placed for adoption. It will be important to have discussed these issues in visits and they are discussed in turn below. Any changes proposed, for instance, to support or contact arrangements, should be confirmed at the next review.

However, visits are vitally important in themselves. There is a salutary reminder of this in the report of a Part 8 Review into the care of a child of four who died in December 1999 (Brighton and Hove ACPC, 2001) while placed for adoption and whose prospective adopters were later imprisoned in relation to his killing. The report states:

> A review is no substitute for continuing effective social work. When the review is perceived as the primary safety net, people easily slip into lesser standards of vigilance and assume the review will pick up anything they have missed. Good practice dictates that reviewing progress, redefining goals, and checking information should be part of every social work interaction, something that happens regularly and systematically, not just at LAC reviews.

While the vast majority of prospective adopters will be doing their very best to parent the child well and need support in doing this, it must not be forgotten that the child's welfare is paramount. In the case mentioned, the adopters commented that they found the social work visits 'intrusive' and 'undermining'. As a result, visits became more low key, to enable the couple to feel less 'scrutinised'. In fact, more rather than less scrutiny was needed.

It will be important to see and talk with both parents, if there are two. Either or both parents may have returned to work and should be seen. He or she may be finding it harder to build a relationship with the child because of spending less time at home. They may also underestimate the challenges the child presents.

It will also be important to ask about any other children in the family and to try to talk to them. How are they adjusting to the new child? Is there any extra help or support they need?

The following are the issues which need addressing, to inform the reviews.

a) Whether the agency remains satisfied that the child should be placed for adoption

There should be confirmation at each review that the adoption by this family of this child is the right thing for the child and the evidence for this needs to be gathered during visits. The child and the adopters may well have some ambivalent feelings in the early weeks and months of a placement as they struggle to get to know each other well and to live together. It will not be helpful to potentially undermine the attachments which it is to be hoped are gradually developing by asking this question too directly. However, during visits you should keep it in mind and be alert to any signs that the child may not be happy or thriving or that the adopters need more help or support and know how to seek and accept support.

b) The child's needs, welfare and development, and whether any changes need to be made to meet the child's needs or assist their development – this will include the arrangements for assessing and meeting the child's health care and educational needs

These are likely to be key areas for discussion during visits. It will be important to listen carefully to any concerns which either the prospective adopters or the child express. It will also be important to be proactive in observing the child and in assessing whether there are any issues which need attending to. Is there anything which you could arrange or provide in relation to meeting the child's health care or educational needs or to enhancing their welfare generally?

c) Existing contact arrangements, whether they should continue or be altered

This is an important topic to discuss in visits. The contact arrangements should be clearly set out in writing. How are they working in practice? Are the child and prospective adopters reasonably happy with them? Are they meeting the child's expressed or perceived needs? Any proposed changes should be confirmed at a review, with an extra one arranged if necessary.

d) Arrangements in relation to the exercise of parental responsibility for the child, and whether they should continue or be altered

The views of the adopter and of the child, if appropriate, should be sought on how this is working out. Adoption Guidance 5.20 suggests that adopters could be given more opportunity to exercise their parental responsibility as their parenting skills develop. They could be given responsibility, for example, for attendance at meetings and involvement in decisions about the child's special educational needs or about therapy. They could also decide about choice of school and about holidays and school trips abroad. The degree to which adopters take on the exercise of parental responsibility before the adoption order will vary and needs to be discussed in each case, rather than adopters being fitted into a uniform system.

e) Adoption support services for the adoptive family and whether there should be any re-assessment of the family's support needs

As adopters actually start parenting a child, it may become clear to them that they need more or different support from that originally planned or arranged. It will be helpful to involve your agency's adoption support worker in any re-assessment of the family's support needs. Families should be aware of adoption support provision and entitlements. You can check that they have the Adoption Passport and are aware of the information on adoption support on the First4Adoption website. If an application to the Adoption Support Fund is being considered, you can begin the preparation work so that the application can be submitted as soon as the adoption order is made.

f) Frequency of social worker visits

As stated earlier, visits must be weekly in the first month, until the first review, and then at such frequency as is decided at that review. There should be discussion with the adopters, and with the child if he or she is old enough, about whether visits should continue weekly or should be more or less frequent for a time. Placements can sometimes become more, rather than less, challenging after an initial "honeymoon" period and it may well be helpful to continue to offer at least weekly visits over the next few months. There should also be discussion about which social worker should visit. If the child is very young and has no relationship with his or her social worker, it may be appropriate for visits from this worker to become less frequent and for the adopter's worker to continue with regular visits.

Reviews after placement

Statutory reviews of looked after children are covered by the Review of Children's Cases Regulations 1991 and The Review of Children's Cases (Amendment) (England) Regulations 2004 up to the point when a local authority is authorised to place a child for adoption.

From the time that a local authority is authorised to place a child for adoption, the requirements for reviews are covered by AAR 36. This regulation requires that, once a child is placed for adoption, reviews must be held:

- not more than four weeks after the date on which the child is placed for adoption;

- not more than three months after the first review;

- and then not more than six months after the date of the previous review.

When carrying out a review, the agency is required by AAR 36 to ascertain the views of:

- the child, having regard to his or her age or understanding;

- the prospective adopter;

- any other person the agency considers relevant. These could include, for instance, other children living in the home, a health visitor, therapist or teacher. It could also include the child's parent or guardian where the agency considers it appropriate.

Birth parents, at this stage, still retain their parental responsibility but their ability to exercise it is limited. Issues around contact should already have been discussed and decisions made. It would be good practice in most cases to ask parents whether they have any view or comments which they would like fed into the review but it is unlikely that they will have anything much to contribute to the review at this stage.

AAR 36.6 sets out the matters which should be considered at the review. These are:

- whether the agency remains satisfied that the child should be placed for adoption;

- the child's needs, welfare and development, and whether any changes need to be made to meet the child's needs or assist their development;

- the existing arrangements for contact, and whether they should continue or be altered;

- the arrangements in relation to the exercise of parental responsibility for the child, and whether they should continue or be altered;

- the arrangements for the provision of adoption support services for the adoptive family and whether there should be any re-assessment of the need for those services;

- in consultation with the appropriate agencies, the arrangements for assessing and meeting the child's health care and educational needs;

- the frequency of social worker visits until the next review;

- the frequency of reviews, subject to the minimum requirements for these.

The Independent Reviewing Officer (IRO) who chairs the review must ensure, as far as is reasonably practicable, that:

- the child's views are understood and taken into account;

- anyone responsible for implementing any decision taken as a result of a review is identified;

- a failure to review the case adequately or to implement the decisions made is brought to the attention of senior managers.

A written record of the review and any decisions must be placed on the child's case record.

A key issue which will need to be discussed and agreed at a review is the timing of the application to court for the adoption order. This is discussed in Chapter 14, *Applying for the adoption order*.

Placements which disrupt

Unfortunately, however carefully the preparation work is done and however hard everyone works to make the placement a success and to support it, some placements do come to a premature end. The research report, *Beyond the Adoption Order* (Selwyn *et al*, 2015), shows that 3.2 per cent of adoptions disrupt after the adoption order, and provides helpful insights. A helpful practice guide on dealing with disruption (Argent and Coleman, 2012) is referenced at the end of this chapter.

Selwyn *et al*'s research found that factors most associated with disruption included:

- older age at placement;

- behaviour difficulties;

- birth family factors such as maltreatment and domestic violence;

- system factors such as delay and lack of support to adoptive families.

FURTHER READING

Argent H and Coleman J (2012) *Dealing with Disruption in Fostering and Adoption Placements* (2nd edn), London: BAAF

Brighton and Hove ACPC (2001) *Report of the Part 8 Review for Brighton and Hove ACPC of the care and protection of JAS (aged 4) who died on 24 December 1999*, Brighton: Brighton and Hove ACPC

Carr K (2007) *Adoption Undone*, London: BAAF

Lilley J (2016) *Our Adoption Journey: A couple's path to adoptive parenthood*, London: CoramBAAF

Selwyn J, Meakings S and Wijedasa D (2015) *Beyond the Adoption Order: Challenges, interventions and adoption disruption*, London: BAAF

Wise J (2007) *Flying Solo: A single parent's adoption story*, London: BAAF

BOOKS FOR USE WITH CHILDREN

Foxon J (2002) *Nutmeg Gets Cross*, London: BAAF

Foxon J (2003) *Nutmeg Gets a Letter*, London: BAAF

Foxon J (2004) *Nutmeg Gets a Little Help*, London: BAAF

Applying for the adoption order

The Adoption and Children Act Section 42 (2) specifies that the child must have had his or her home with the applicant, or with one or both of them if they are a couple, at all times during the ten weeks preceding the application to court.

In fact, many prospective adopters may wait longer than this before applying to court. You and the family's social worker will need to discuss the timing of an application to court with them during visits and a decision to go ahead should usually be confirmed at a review.

The adopters and the child will need to feel ready to make the permanent legal commitment of adoption. However, the support arrangements you have agreed will probably extend beyond the making of an adoption order and so prospective adopters no longer need to feel ready to go it alone before applying to adopt: adopters can apply to the Adoption Support Fund for certain types of support and you could have the application ready to submit as soon as the adoption order is made.

Making the application

The application can be made to a local Magistrates' Family Proceedings Court, to a County Court which deals with adoption (now a network of designated adoption centres), or to the High Court.

Your legal department should be able to advise on which court would be most appropriate.

The prospective adopters should get and complete an application form. They may need information from your records to enable them to complete it. They will have to supply the child's birth certificate and copies of court orders. A court fee will be payable. Most local authorities will pay this fee. They must disregard means when considering paying the court fee (Adoption Guidance 9.36).

The court report

The Family Procedure (Adoption) Rules 2005, Rule 29, specifies that a report must be submitted 'on the suitability of the applicant to adopt a child'.

The details of what this report must cover are specified in a Practice Direction to the Rules, in Annex A. So, the court report is sometimes called a Rule 29 report and sometimes an Annex A report. They are the same thing.

The report can be written by several people, for example, you, as the child's worker and the prospective adopter's worker (see the section in Chapter 1 on who can write adoption reports).

Annex A sets out clear headings for each section of the report. It will be a good idea to discuss it with your adoption team, who will have experience of completing these reports. You could also discuss any particular issues you have with your legal department. You will already have gathered a lot of the information, in your CPR, adoption placement report and plan and in your visits to the family and reviews of the placement. The prospective adopter's worker will have information on them in the prospective adopter's report.

The court will give directions on the timing of the report, and on any other matters to be dealt with before the final adoption hearing, e.g. the child's attendance at court.

What is the legal effect of an adoption order?

This is set out in s.46 of the Adoption and Children Act.

- An adoption order extinguishes parental responsibility which any person other than the adopters has and gives full parental responsibility for the child to the adopters. The birth parents cease to be the child's parents in law and have no further legal rights or responsibilities in relation to the child.

- Any order made under the 1989 Act is extinguished, such as a special guardianship order or care order, as is a placement order.

- If the child has been adopted before and that placement has broken down, this adoption order will extinguish the parental rights and responsibilities of those former adoptive parents.

Leave to oppose an adoption order

If there is a placement order, can birth parents oppose the making of the adoption order?

Section 47 of the Adoption and Children Act specifies that a parent may not oppose the making of an adoption order without the leave of the court. The court cannot give leave unless it is satisfied that there has been a change of circumstances since the placement order was made.

Case law has held that in an application for leave to oppose under s.47, there is a two-stage process (*Adoption & Fostering*, Volume 31:3, 2007).

- The court has first to consider whether there has been a change in circumstances. For example, a parent may have completed successful drug rehabilitation.

- The judge will then consider whether, if the change were sufficient, he or she should exercise discretion and give leave. The judge will need to bear in mind the requirements of s.1 of the Adoption and Children Act, including the welfare checklist. Section 1 lays down that the child's welfare, throughout his or her life, is the paramount consideration. So, even if the judge decides that there has been a change of circumstances, he or she may still exercise their discretion and not grant leave to oppose the order.

- If the judge considers that leave should not be granted, he or she will not usually make the adoption order at that point but will allow a period for the birth parent to appeal.

If there is a formal CAFCASS-witnessed consent, can birth parents oppose the making of the adoption order?

The process is exactly the same as when there is a placement order, as described in the previous section.

What happens if leave to oppose the making of an adoption order is granted?

The court must first decide whether an adoption order is in the child's best interests. It must then decide whether or not to dispense with parental consent to adoption.

If leave has been granted by the court, under s.47, for a parent or guardian to oppose the making of the final adoption order, the parents may apply for a child arrangements order and the guardian may apply for a special guardianship order, to be considered at the final adoption order hearing, as an alternative to the proposed adoption.

If the adoption application is going to be contested in court you will need to take advice from your legal department. The adopters may also need to be legally represented. The local authority will usually pay the adopter's legal costs and must disregard their means when considering this (Adoption Guidance 9.36).

Consent and dispensing with consent

Adoption orders cannot be made unless:

- *each parent or guardian consents to the making of the order; or*

- *consent to placement for adoption has previously been given under Section 19 of the ACA 2002 and has not been withdrawn; or*

- *the child is subject to a placement order; or*

- *the court dispenses with consent* (Cullen and Lane, 2006).

If there is a placement order or consent under s.19, the issue of consent does not need to be looked at again *unless* the parent is given leave to oppose the adoption. Since 2013, there has been an increase in the number of cases granted leave to appeal, but CoramBAAF is aware of only one case where an adoption order has not been made after the appeal has been considered.

Dispensing with parental consent to the making of an adoption order

The court may dispense with the consent of a parent or guardian to the making of an adoption order on the grounds that:

- the parent cannot be found;

- the parent is incapable of consenting; or

- the welfare of the child requires their consent to be dispensed with.

Contact issues

Section 46(6) of the Adoption and Children Act imposes a duty on the court to consider the existing and proposed arrangements for contact with the child, and to seek the views of the parties to the proceedings on these arrangements.

The court can make a contact order or a no contact order, under s.51 of the 1989 Children Act, if it considers this to be in the best interests of the child. However, there is no presumption in favour of contact. At all times, the child's welfare is the paramount consideration.

You will already have had extensive discussion with the birth parents and others, with the adopters and with the child, about contact (see Chapter 6, *Contact*). It is to be hoped that some agreement has been reached and that there are no surprises at this stage.

Children as parties to proceedings

The child will only be made a party in certain circumstances set out in the court rules. If the child is made a party (for instance, if there is a dispute about contact) then he or she will have a CAFCASS guardian and a solicitor unless the court consider this unnecessary. The court may ask a CAFCASS officer to prepare a welfare report on the child. The writer of such a report is referred to in the rules as 'children and family reporter'.

Parent or guardian in adoption law

- "Parent" means each birth parent with parental responsibility for the child. (It would include a step-parent who has adopted the child but not one who has acquired parental responsibility through a parental responsibility agreement or order or through a residence order.)

- "Special Guardian" means someone who has a special guardianship order,

- "Guardian" means someone who has been appointed to act in the place of a parent after their death. Only a parent with parental responsibility may appoint a guardian. The appointment will usually only take effect after the death of both parents with parental responsibility. The exception is if the parent who appointed the guardian had a child arrangements order before their death. In this case, the guardian acquires parental responsibility even though the other parent may still be alive.

Using these definitions, these are the people who must be counselled and consulted about adoption plans and whose consent must be sought. Birth fathers without parental responsibility should be counselled if the agency thinks this is appropriate. This is discussed in more detail in Chapter 3. However, their consent to adoption is not a legal requirement.

Court hearing

Unless the parents have consented to a specific adoption under s.20 and have said that they do not wish to be notified of the final hearing, the court must notify them of the application. They will also be notified of the Directions hearing. Different courts have their own practice in relation to who attends court and when. Many try to ensure that birth parents, if they wish to attend, are not at the same hearing as the adopters and child. You will need to take advice from your legal department on this.

Whether or not the child is made a party to the proceedings, the Court Rules require that he or she must attend court before the order is made, unless the court has decided that this is not necessary.

The court will usually try to make arrangements for this to be a happy occasion for the child and adopters, once it is satisfied that there is not likely to be any legal bar to granting the order.

Different courts have different ways of approaching these hearings and it is important for you, with the help of your legal department, to find out what the local practice is.

Although there may well be ongoing support to the family and ongoing contact arrangements, the granting of an adoption order is still a significant event for the child and the adopters.

> *I love reading the ending of a book because of the feeling of triumph that you've finished it ... and I guess that was the same feeling in court, watching them close the book, really shutting it ... Knowing that nothing else was going to happen. It was just going to be an ordinary life from now on.* (Girl quoted in Thomas and Beckford, 1999.)

After adoption

The child will be issued with new certificates to take the place of the original birth certificate. The new short certificate will be the same as if the child was born to the adopters (assuming that he or she takes their surname). The long certificate is again in the new name but does make clear that it is an adoption certificate.

Records

The child's adoption file must be kept securely for 100 years from the date of the adoption order. The child at 18 can request access to information from it and has a right to everything which his or her adoptive parents were given on placement. It will need to be made clear in the record exactly what they were given.

FURTHER READING

National Adoption Leadership Board (2014) *Impact of Court Judgements on Adoption: What the judgements do and do not say*, available at: www.first4adoption.org.uk/wp-content/uploads/2014/11/ALB-Impact-of-Court-Judgments-on-Adoption-November-2014.pdf

Thomas C and Beckford V with Lowe N and Murch M (1999) *Adopted Children Speaking*, London: BAAF

BOOKS FOR USE WITH CHILDREN

Argent H and Lane M (2003) *What Happens in Court? A guide for children*, London: BAAF

References

Argent H and Coleman J (2012) *Dealing with Disruption in Fostering and Adoption Placements* (2nd edn), London: BAAF

Argent H (2006) *Ten Top Tips for Placing Children*, London: BAAF

BAAF (1996) *Planning for Permanence*, Practice Note 33, London: BAAF

Beesley P (2015) *Making Good Assessments*, London: BAAF

Bond H (2007) *Ten Top Tips for Managing Contact*, London: BAAF

Brighton and Hove ACPC (2001) *Report of the Part 8 Review for Brighton and Hove ACPC of the care and protection of JAS (aged 4) who died on 24 December 1999*, Brighton: Brighton and Hove ACPC

Commission for Social Care Inspection (2006) *Adoption – Messages from Inspections of Adoption Agencies*, London: CSCI

Cullen D and Conroy Harris A (2014) *Child Care Law: England and Wales*, London: BAAF

Department for Education (2015a) *Special Guardianship: A call for views*, available at: www.gov.uk/government/consultations/special-guardianship-review

Department for Education (2015b) *Early Permanence Placements and the Approval of Prospective Adopters as Foster Carers*, London: DfE

Department for Education (2015c) *Guidance and Regulations Volume 2: Care planning, placement and case review*, London: DfE

Department for Education (2016a) *Adoption: A vision for change*, available at: www.gov.uk/government/publications/adoption-a-vision-for-change

Department for Education (2016b) *Children's Social Care Reform: A vision for change*, available at: www.gov.uk/government/publications/childrens-social-care-reform-a-vision-for-change

Department of Health (2000) *Framework for the Assessment of Children in Need and their Families*, London: Department of Health

Department of Health and Welsh Assembly Government (2003) *Adoption: National Minimum Standards*, London: The Stationery Office

Hall A (2008) *Special Guardianship and Permanency Planning: A missed opportunity?*, unpublished dissertation, London

Lefevre M (2008) 'Knowing, being and doing: core qualities and skills for working with children and young people in care' in Luckock B and Lefevre M (eds) *Direct Work: Social work with children and young people*, London: BAAF

Morgan R (2006) *About Adoption: A children's views report*, London: CSCI. Also on www.rights4me.org

National Adoption Leadership Board (2014) *Impact of Court Judgements on Adoption: What the judgements do and do not say*, available at: www.first4adoption.org.uk/wp-content/uploads/2014/11/ALB-Impact-of-Court-Judgments-on-Adoption-November-2014.pdf

Sellick C and Thoburn J (1996) *What Works in Family Placement?*, London: Barnardo's

Thomas C and Beckford V with Lowe N and Murch M (1999) *Adopted Children Speaking*, London: BAAF

Selwyn J, Meakings S and Wijedasa D (2015) *Beyond the Adoption Order,* London: BAAF

Wade J, Sinclair I, Stuttard L and Simmonds J (2014) *Investigating Special Guardianship: Experiences, challenges and outcomes*, London: DfE, available at: www.gov.uk/government/uploads/system/uploads/attachment_data/file/377448/DFE-RR372_Investigating_special_guardianship.pdf

Wade J, Dixon J and Richards A (2010) *Special Guardianship in Practice*, London: BAAF

Appendix 1

National Minimum Standards for Adoption – Values Statement

The values statement below is included in the introduction to the Standards and explains the important principles which underpin them. These values complement the crucially important requirements in s.1 of the Adoption and Children Act 2002 (as amended by the Children and Families Act 2014), the "welfare checklist", and should be kept in mind in your work with children and families.

Values

- The child's welfare, safety and needs are at the centre of the adoption process.

- Adopted children should have an enjoyable childhood, and benefit from excellent parenting and education, enjoying a wide range of opportunities to develop their talents and skills leading to a successful adult life.

- Children are entitled to grow up as part of a loving family that can meet their developmental needs during childhood and beyond.

- Children's wishes and feelings are important and will be actively sought and fully taken into account at all stages of the adoption process.

- Delays should be avoided as they can have a severe impact on the health and development of the children waiting to be adopted.

- A sense of identity is important to a child's well-being. To help children develop this, their ethnic origin, cultural background, religion, language and sexuality need to be properly recognised and positively valued and promoted.

- The particular needs of disabled children and children with complex needs will be fully recognised and taken into account.

- Where a child cannot be cared for in a suitable manner in their own country, intercountry adoption may be considered as an alternative means of providing a permanent family.

- Children, birth parents/guardians and families and adoptive parents and families will be valued and respected.

- A genuine partnership between all those involved in adoption is essential for the NMS to deliver the best outcomes for children; this includes the Government, local government, other statutory agencies, Voluntary Adoption Agencies and Adoption Support Agencies.

Reproduced from Department for Education (2014) *Adoption: National minimum standards*, London: DfE

Appendix 2

Adoption and Children Act 2002

The Children and Families Act 2014 makes a number of amendments to s.1 of the 2002 Act. For adoption agencies in England the main change is the repeal of subsection 5, which has been deleted in the following extract.

Section 1

(1) This section applies whenever a court or adoption agency is coming to a decision relating to the adoption of a child.

(2) The paramount consideration of the court or adoption agency must be the child's welfare, throughout his life.

(3) The court or adoption agency must at all times bear in mind that, in general, any delay in coming to the decision is likely to prejudice the child's welfare.

(4) The court or adoption agency must have regard to the following matters (among others) –

    (a) the child's ascertainable wishes and feelings regarding the decision (considered in the light of the child's age and understanding),

    (b) the child's particular needs,

    (c) the likely effect on the child (throughout his life) of having ceased to be a member of the original family and become an adopted person,

    (d) the child's age, sex, background and any of the child's characteristics which the court or agency considers relevant,

    (e) any harm (within the meaning of the Children Act 1989 (c. 41)) which the child has suffered or is at risk of suffering,

    (f) the relationship which the child has with relatives, and with any other person in relation to whom the court or agency considers the relationship to be relevant, including –

        (i) the likelihood of any such relationship continuing and the value to the child of its doing so,

        (ii) the ability and willingness of any of the child's relatives, or of any such person, to provide the child with a secure environment in which the child can develop, and otherwise to meet the child's needs,

        (iii) the wishes and feelings of any of the child's relatives, or of any such person, regarding the child.

(6) In coming to a decision relating to the adoption of a child, a court or adoption agency must always consider the whole range of powers available to it in the child's case (whether under this Act or the Children Act 1989); and the court must not make any order under this Act unless it considers that making the order would be better for the child than not doing so.

(7) In this section, "coming to a decision relating to the adoption of a child", in relation to a court, includes –

(a) coming to a decision in any proceedings where the orders that might be made by the court include an adoption order (or the revocation of such an order), a placement order (or the revocation of such an order) or an order under section 26 (or the revocation or variation of such an order),

(b) coming to a decision about granting leave in respect of any action (other than the initiation of proceedings in any court) which may be taken by an adoption agency or individual under this Act, but does not include coming to a decision about granting leave in any other circumstances.

(8) For the purposes of this section –

(a) references to relationships are not confined to legal relationships,

(b) references to a relative, in relation to a child, include the child's mother and father.

Reproduced from *Adoption and Children Act 2002* (Ch.38), London: The Stationery Office, as amended by the Children and Families Act 2014.

Appendix 3

Glossary of terms

Accommodated/Accommodation

Under Section 20 of the Children Act 1989 the local authority is required to 'provide accommodation' for children 'in need' in certain circumstances. The local authority does not acquire parental responsibility (see below) merely by accommodating a child and the arrangements for the child must normally be agreed with the parent(s), who, subject to certain restrictions, are entitled to remove the children from local authority accommodation at any time.

Adoption agency

A local authority or a voluntary adoption agency.

Adoption order

An adoption order transfers parental responsibility for the child from birth parents and others who had parental responsibility, including the local authority, permanently and solely to the adopters. The child is deemed to be the child of the adopters as if she or he had been born to them. Any order made under the 1989 Children Act, such as a residence order or a special guardianship order, is extinguished, as is a placement order or contact order made under the Adoption and Children Act (see also the section on adoption in Chapter 1, *Making a permanence plan*).

Adoption placement plan

A plan that gives information to the prospective adopter about the child when the agency has decided to place the child with them. It sets out, for example, when the child will move into the prospective adopter's home, parental responsibility, adoption support services, contact with the child, and arrangements for reviewing the placement.

Adoption placement report

A report prepared by the adoption agency for the adoption panel which sets out, for example, the reasons for proposing the placement, arrangements for allowing any person contact with the child, the prospective adopter's view on the proposed placement, and, where the agency is a local authority, proposals for providing adoption support services for the adoptive family.

Adoption Register

A database of approved prospective adopters and children waiting for adoption across England. A team of experienced social workers will use the database to link children with approved prospective adopters where local matches cannot be found. The Adoption Register also arranges Adoption Exchange Days where approved adopters can find out about children needing adoption and meet their social workers.

Adoption Support Agency (ASA)

An organisation or person registered, under Part 2 of the Care Standards Act 2000, to provide adoption support services. An ASA may operate on a profit, or not-for-profit basis.

Adoption support services

Support, including financial support; services to enable adopted children, adoptive parents and birth parents to discuss matters relating to adoption; assistance including mediation services in relation to contact between the adopted child and birth family; therapeutic services for adopted children; assistance for the purpose of ensuring the continuance of the relationship between an adoptive child and his or her adoptive parent; assistance where disruption of an adoptive placement or adoption arrangement following an adoption order has occurred or is in danger of occurring; intermediary services, counselling, advice and information in relation to adoption.

Agency adviser

A senior member of the agency's staff who is a social worker with at least five years' relevant post-qualifying experience and relevant management experience. The agency adviser attends adoption panel meetings, provides advice to the panel and maintains an overview of the quality of the agency's reports to the adoption panel.

Agency decision-maker

A senior member of the agency's staff who makes decisions on behalf of the agency, having received a recommendation and advice from the adoption panel, as to whether a child should be placed for adoption with a particular prospective adopter.

Article 15 report

Report prepared on the prospective adopter under Article 15 of the Convention on Protection of Children and Co-operation in respect of Intercountry Adoption (the Hague Convention). This includes information on their identity, eligibility and suitability to adopt, background, family and medical history, social environment, reasons for adoption, ability to undertake an intercountry adoption and the characteristics of the children for whom they would be qualified to care.

Article 16 information

Report prepared on the child under Article 16 of the Hague Convention. This includes information on his or her identity, adoptability, background, social environment, family history, medical history including that of the child's family, and any special needs of the child.

Authority to place for adoption

An adoption agency is authorised to place a child for adoption when it has a placement order made under Section 21 of the Adoption and Children Act or the formal consent of the child's parents or guardians under Section 19 of the Adoption and Children Act.

CAFCASS

The Children and Family Court Advisory and Support Service is a national non-departmental public body for England. It has brought together the services provided by the Family Court Welfare Service, the Guardian *ad Litem* Services and the Children's Division of the Official Solicitor. CAFCASS is independent of the courts, social services, education and health authorities and all similar agencies.

CAMHS (Child and Adolescent Mental Health Services)

Services that contribute to the mental health care of children and young people, whether provided by health, education, social services or other agencies. CAMHS cover all types of provision and intervention from mental health promotion and primary prevention and specialist community-based services through to very specialist care as provided by in-patient units for young people with mental illness.

Child arrangements order

An order made under s.12 of the Children and Adoption Act 2014 which amends s.8(1) of the Children Act 1989. It states: 'A child arrangements order means an order regulating arrangements relating to any of the following-

a) With whom a child is to live, spend time or otherwise have contact, and

b) When a child is to live, spend time or otherwise have contact with any person.'

Children's guardian

A person working for CAFCASS who is appointed by the court to safeguard a child's interests in court proceedings.

Child's case record

This file must be set up when an adoption agency is considering adoption for a child. The information to be kept on it is set out in AAR12.1 and AIR4

Child's permanence report

A report prepared by the adoption agency. This will include, for example, information about the child and his or her family, a summary of the state of the child's health, his or her health history and any need for health care; wishes and feelings of the child, his or her parent or guardian; the agency's view about the child's need for contact with his or her parents, guardian or any other person the agency considers relevant.

Concurrent planning (see also Fostering for Adoption)

A term used to describe the placement of a child for whom a local authority is considering adoption with approved adopters who are also approved foster carers. The placement may be made before or after the ADM decision for adoption.

Consortium

A group of usually not more than six–eight local adoption agencies, which share details of waiting families and children in order to try to make speedy local placements for children.

Contact

Allowing a person contact with the child to be placed for adoption. Contact may take the form of *indirect* contact, letters and cards, and background information on the child's progress being sent via a social worker. In some cases there may be some form of *direct* contact where the child visits or stays with a particular person.

Contact order (see child arrangements order)

Couple

Two people (whether of different sexes or the same sex) living as partners (married, unmarried or in a civil partnership) in an enduring family relationship. This does not include two people one of whom is the other's parent, grandparent, sister, brother, aunt or uncle (Adoption and Children Act s144(4)).

DBS (Disclosure and Barring Service)

A non-departmental public body of the Home Office which provides access to criminal records and other information to organisations to help them make informed decisions. In the context of adoption, the DBS provides enhanced disclosures on prospective adopters and adult members of their household which assist the adoption agency in their assessment of a prospective adopter's suitability to adopt a child. It also provides enhanced disclosures on panel members.

Form E

The CoramBAAF form which used to be used to record information on a child for whom adoption was the plan. It has now been replaced by the Child's Permanence Report.

Form F

The CoramBAAF form which used to be used to record information on prospective adopters. It has now been replaced by the Prospective Adopter's Report. This report must be compiled and presented to the adoption panel when the suitability to adopt of prospective adopters is being considered.

Fostering/foster care

In this book, this term is used for those cases where a child is placed with a foster carer approved by the local authority (under Section 23(2)(a) Children Act 1989) or (in rare cases) placed directly by a voluntary organisation (under Section 59(1)(a) of the Act). These placements are governed by the Fostering Services Regulations 2002. "Short-term", "long-term", and "permanent" foster care and "respite care" (also known as "short breaks") may mean different things to different people; they are not legally defined terms.

Fostering for Adoption

A term used to describe the placement of a child for whom a local authority is considering adoption with approved adopters who are also approved foster carers. The placement may be made before or after the ADM decision for adoption.

Freeing order

A court order dealing with the parents' consent to adoption and freeing a child for adoption. Freeing orders can no longer be applied for but existing orders remain in force. A freeing order allows the child to be placed for adoption. The prospective adopters will not have parental responsibility. The court considering making an adoption order will not need to consider the parents' consent as this has already been considered and dealt with.

Guardian

Not to be confused with a children's guardian or a special guardian. A guardian is a person who has been appointed to act in the place of a parent after their death. The guardian will usually only assume parental responsibility after the death of a surviving parent with parental responsibility. The guardian must be consulted at all stages of the adoption process and has the right to consent or withhold consent to placement for adoption.

In care

A child who is subject to a care order under Section 31 of the Children Act 1989 is described as being 'in care'. A care order gives the local authority parental responsibility for the child but does not deprive the birth parent(s) of this. Nevertheless, the local authority may limit the extent to which parents may exercise their parental responsibility and may override parental wishes in the interests of the child's welfare.

Independent Review Mechanism (IRM)

A review process that is conducted by an independent review panel. The prospective adopter may initiate this process when their adoption agency has made a qualifying determination about their suitability to adopt. The review panel reviews the case and gives a fresh recommendation to the agency.

Independent Reviewing Officer (IRO)

The IRO must chair statutory child care reviews and ensure that reviews are timely. They must monitor the effectiveness, appropriateness and implementation of care plans. They are required to be independent of the management of the case and of the allocation of resources.

Looked after

This term includes both children "in care" and accommodated children. Local authorities have certain duties towards all looked after children and their parents, which are set out in Part III and Schedule 2 of the Children Act 1989. These include the duty to safeguard and promote the child's welfare and the duty to consult with children and parents before taking decisions.

Ofsted

Ofsted has responsibility for the regulation and inspection of all children's services.

Open adoption

This term may be used very loosely and can mean anything from an adoption where a child continues to have frequent face-to-face contact with members of his or her birth family to an adoption where there is some degree of "openness", e.g. the birth family and adopters meeting each other once. People using the term should be asked to define what they mean!

Parental responsibility (PR)

Parental responsibility is defined by the Children Act 1989 as 'all the rights, duties, powers, responsibilities and authority which by law a parent of a child has in relation to the child and his or her property'. The most important elements of parental responsibility include:

- providing a home for the child;
- having contact with the child;
- protecting and maintaining the child;
- disciplining the child;
- determining and providing for the child's education;
- determining the religion of the child;
- consenting to the child's medical treatment;
- naming the child or agreeing to the child's change of name;
- consenting to or withholding consent to placement for adoption and adoption.

Parallel or twin-track planning

When work in relation to rehabilitation home to parents and preliminary work about other permanent options for the child are done at the same time.

Placement order

An order made by the court under Section 21 of the Adoption and Children Act 2002 authorising a local authority to place a child for adoption with any prospective adopters who may be chosen by the authority. It continues in force until it is revoked, or an adoption order is made in respect of the child, or the child marries, forms a civil partnership or attains the age of 18. Only local authorities may apply for placement orders.

Prospective adopter

A person who has applied to be an adoptive parent. The term tends to be used until the making of the adoption order.

Prospective adopter's report

A report prepared by the adoption agency.

- full report – includes, for example, the prospective adopter's date of birth, identifying information, racial origin, cultural/linguistic background, religious persuasion, description of his or her personality, whether he or she is single or a member of a couple, the agency's assessment of his or her suitability to adopt a child, and a summary of the prospective adopter's state of health.

- Brief report – the agency does not need to complete a full report where it receives information that leads it to consider that the prospective adopter may not be suitable to adopt a child. That information would be that either set out in Part 1, Schedule 4 of the AAR, or the health report, or report of interview with referees, or the local authority report, or other information.

Residence order

An order under Section 8 of the Children Act 1989 settling the arrangements as to the person(s) with whom the child is to live. Where a residence order is made in favour of someone who does not already have parental responsibility for the child (e.g. a relative or foster carer), that person will acquire parental responsibility subject to certain restrictions (e.g. they will not be able to consent to the child's adoption). Parental responsibility given in connection with a residence order will only last as long as the residence order. A residence order can last until the child's 18th birthday. The Children and Families Act 2014 replaced residence orders with child arrangements orders.

Residence order allowance

Local authorities have a power (under Schedule 1 Para 15 of the 1989 Children Act) to contribute to the cost of a child's maintenance when the child is living with somebody under a residence order provided he or she is not living with a parent or step-parent. A financial contribution under this power is normally referred to as a residence order allowance.

Section 8 order

An order made under Section 8 of the 1989 Children Act. These orders are a prohibited steps order and a specific issue order. Under the Children and Families Act 2014, contact and residence orders have been replaced by a child arrangements order.

Section 84 order

An order made under Section 84 of the Adoption and Children Act. It authorises a prospective adopter to remove a child from the British Islands for the purpose of adoption in another country.

Special guardianship

An order made under the Adoption and Children Act 2002 offering an alternative legal status for children. The child is no longer looked after. It gives the special guardian parental responsibility which he or she can exercise to the exclusion of others. However, the birth parent(s) retain parental responsibility. Support services, including financial support, are very similar to those for adopters.

Appendix 4

Useful organisations

CoramBAAF
41 Brunswick Square
London WC1N 1AZ
Tel: 020 7520 7515
www.corambaaf.org.uk

Adoption Register for England
Unit 4, Pavilion Business Park
Royds Hall Road, Wortley
Leeds LS12 6AJ
Tel: 0870 750 2173
www.adoptionregister.org.uk

Adoption UK
Linden House
55 The Green
South Bar Street
Banbury OX16 9AB
Tel: 01295 752240
www.adoptionuk.org

Children who Wait magazine
A family-finding service run by Adoption UK
Contact details as above

Department for Education (DfE)
The Adoption Team
Sanctuary Buildings
Great Smith Street
London SW1P 3BT
Tel: 0370 000 2288
www.gov.uk/government/organisations/
department-for-education

Family Rights Group (FRG)
A national organisation which advises families
which are in contact with social services about
the care of their children.
The Print House
18 Ashwin Street
London E8 3DL
Tel: 0808 801 0366
www.frg.org.uk

First4Adoption
National information service for people
interested in adopting a child in England.
Provides links to adoption agencies and VAAs.
48 Mecklenburgh Square
London WC1N 2QA
Email: helpdesk@first4adoption.org.uk
Tel: 0300 222 0022
www.first4adoption.org.uk

Fostering Network
87 Blackfriars Road
London SE1 8HA
Tel: 020 7620 6400
www.thefosteringnetwork.org.uk

Fosterline
An advice and information service for foster
carers and those interested in fostering,
funded by the DfE and delivered by FosterTalk.
87 Blackfriars Road
London SE1 8HA
Tel: 0800 040 7675
Email: enquiries@fosterline.info
www.fosterline.info

Foster Talk
An advice and information service for foster
carers.
Tel: 01527 836910
www.fostertalk.org.uk

Intercountry Adoption Centre
Provides independent information and advice
to anyone in the UK considering adopting
a child from abroad, to adoptive families,
adopted people and adoption professionals.
64–66 High Street
Barnet
Herts EN5 5SJ
Tel: 0870 516 8742
www.icacentre.org.uk

Link Maker
Family-finding website service: Adoption Link for adopters, and Placement Link for foster carers.
Tel: 0843 886 0040
www.linkmaker.co.uk

Natural Parents Network (NPN)
National self-help organisation for birth parents who have parted with a child for adoption, run by birth parents. Provides information, support and counselling. Publishes a regular newsletter.
20 Rookery Way
Seaford BN25 2TE
Tel: 0845 456 5031
www.n-p-n.co.uk

POST-ADOPTION AND AFTER ADOPTION CENTRES

Listed are some organisations offering advice, counselling, information, training, and self-help and support groups to adopted people, birth families and adoptive families.

After Adoption
Unit 5 Citygate
5 Blantyre Street
Manchester
M15 4JJ
Tel: 0161 839 4932
Helpline: 0800 056 8578
www.afteradoption.org.uk
After Adoption has a number of regional offices in England and Wales.

New Family Social
The UK network for LGBT (lesbian, gay, bisexual and transgender) adoptive and foster families.
Harvey's Barn
Park End, Swaffham Bulbeck
CB25 0NA
Tel: 0843 2899457
Email: membership@newfamilysocial.co.uk
www.newfamilysocial.org.uk

Post-Adoption Centre (PAC-UK)
London office
5 Torriano Mews
Torriano Avenue
London NW5 2RZ
Tel: 020 7284 5879
www.pac-uk.org

Leeds office
Hollyshaw House
2 Hollyshaw Lane
Leeds LS15 7BD
Tel: 0113 264 6837